A COMFORT BREEZE

A DRAMA-DY
IN THREE ACTS

By Frank Steele

Shojai & Steele Plays
P.O. Box 1904, Sherman, TX 75091
shojai-steele-plays@shojai.com   website: amyshojai.com/plays

***Adult language and themes. Dialogue changes
require advance author approval.***

Performance rights for all materials contained herein
Must be obtained from Shojai & Steele Plays
Copyright © 2008, 2012, 2016 by Frank Steele
Email: Shojai-steele-plays@shojai.com
Website: AmyShojai.com/Plays
ALL RIGHTS RESERVED

A COMFORT BREEZE

CHARACTERS

JOETTA MOSS………………………..……...AGED 47

AUDIE, HER DAUGHTER……………..….AGED 30

SETTING: *1993, summer, a cheap motel room in West Texas. The motel room was nice twenty years ago, but it has seen better days.*

Downstage stage left wall contains tiny windows (open) with water stained curtains. Upstage left is the door, a light switch on the wall next to it.

Stage right wall, center, door leading to bathroom. Upstage of door, chest of drawers (every drawer sticks), with box fan and ice bucket on top.

Downstage of bathroom door, a plain desk/table with a lamp, and two typical hotel chairs. A mirror mounted on the wall above.

Upstage center against wall, double bed with thread-snagged chenille bedspread. Bad painting of mountain scene bolted to wall above headboard. On each side, lights are bolted into the wall.

Nightstands on both sides of bed. One nightstand holds phone without dial, the other an old radio, an ashtray anda bible. Furniture is cigarette burned.

ACT I

Lights up as Joetta Moss enters. She's smoking a cigarette, carrying an old, out of date suitcase, and she's wearing a business suit that was in fashion fifteen years earlier. Joetta is rough, and she's seen more of "life" than most women. She dresses in what she thinks will look good for the occasion. Her taste is somewhat cheap. Her hair is dyed, but the roots show, and she takes nothing from anyone. Joetta is pure west Texas. She has traveled around, but nothing can change what she is. One of the hallmarks of Joetta is how quickly she changes moods. This is for self-protection. She's had to do this all of her life. This is not the Waldorf, and even Joetta knows the difference.

JOETTA

(*Upset. Dropping her suitcase, looking around the room slowly, and picking up the phone*) What in the hell are you trying to do to me? This goddamn room, that's what I mean...Listen, you said this was a deluxe suite....I've been in gas station shitters that were cleaner. Don't tell me to talk nicer. I'll talk any goddamn way I wanna talk. Listen, you get me a better room, or I'm gonna come up there, and kick your coffee-drinkin' ass. OK...OK...OK, look...Don't tell me to calm down. YOU calm down! Just find me somethin' better, real fast, real nice, and real soon. OK, I'll wait. I'LL WAIT. I said I would. Just call me back...No, I'm expectin' someone... None of your damn business. If she shows up, just send her down here. OK... All right...I'm still gonna wait for that call. Yes. Fine, fine, OK. I SAID, "OK". Bellboy? I know you don't have a damn bellboy. I carried this shit down here by myself, and I'll carry this shit to my NEXT DELUXE GODDAMN SUITE by myself, too. (*She hangs up*) Bell boy, my ass...Stupid bastard. (*goes into the bathroom, and comes back with a motel glass. She picks up the phone once more*) This is Joetta Moss again. No, I didn't expect the room change this fast. No, all I need is to know is where the ice machine is. Next to what Coke machine? Well, if I'd seen the Coke machine, then I'd know where the ice machine was, wouldn't I? You'll bring some down? You? You'll bring some down? There's no one to carry suitcases, but there IS someone to carry ice? Well, by god, you do have a point. Ice is lighter than suitcases. *(She laughs a 'cigarette' laugh)* OK, Sugar, whenever the mood hits ya, or whenever you think about it. And, oh, oh, I still want that room!

> *She slowly moves around the room, lights a cigarette, and picks up the suitcase. She sets it on the bed. The first thing she puts away is a safety razor, which she carefully places in the bedside table drawer. Her clothes that are packed are like the ones she wears, cheap and out of style. The faucet drips, and the room is generally just unpleasant. There is a knock at the*

A COMFORT BREEZE

door. Joetta moves slowly to the door and opens it.

Hello? *(She looks around)* Hello. Well, I'll be damned. *(She picks up the ice bucket and sets it on the table next to the bed. She picks up the phone.)*

Lissin, did you just deliver this ice? Yeah, yeah, that's the one. Well, it's already meltin'. Look…I know, I know. How in the hell am I spoze to cool it down with a box fan? The room's ninety degrees! I know it's gonna cool down at night, but what am I spoze ta do until then? Goddammit, I saw Satan standin' outside the room next to me fannin' himself. Does that tell ya somethin'? That maybe your rooms need air conditionin', that's what. All right, OK, let me know. I'm too tired to argue, that's all. Just let me know.

She hangs up, mixes herself a drink, and turns on the room radio. After much static, she picks up a station playing a lot of "older" country songs. She sits and drinks slowly, and taps her foot. "Hey, Good Lookin'" comes on)

You're a little late on that one, darlin'. Where were you thirty years ago?

Joetta looks in the mirror, smiles a smile that says her mind is many years away. She tries to turn the box fan on, but it's broken. As she hits the side of it, she moves back to the chair, and sits down. She takes off her shoes, and loosens her blouse. There is a knock at the door.

Well, it's about damn time. *(There is another knock)* Hold on. It's not easy walkin' through puddles of sweat! *(Once again, there's a knock)* Dammit, Buster. I said, 'I'm comin'.

She opens the door, and is speechless. Audilia is standing there, the daughter she's not seen since birth. Audilia (Audie) is an attractive, stylish woman of thirty. She wears expensive clothes, carries an Aigner briefcase, a leather suitcase, and is way over-dressed for where she is. She looks like 'money', and isn't afraid to show it. She wears a diamond Rolex loosely fitted on her wrist so it won't be covered up by her sleeve. Audie's life is ruled by affectation. She likes being noticed, and will spend whatever it takes to be the center of attention. She speaks in a warm southern drawl which is by design rather than by region. She has manufactured herself into what she is, and nothing has been left to chance. Though cold, Audie can appear friendly, even "giving" at times, but she is always "guarded" and her mood changes reflect her past. She takes pride in that she never gives herself away. There is an awkward pause as

A COMFORT BREEZE

the two women look at each other, neither wanting to speak first.

AUDIE

May I come in?

JOETTA

Yeah, I mean yes, sure. You bet, come on in. (*Audie enters looking around the room. She puts her suitcase and briefcase on the bed. She looks at everything as if it were made of dirt*) Well, it's not the Ramada Inn, but I've been in a lot worse, haven't you? Have a seat. Take a load off, as they say. Let me turn off this radio.

AUDIE

Thank you. (*After dusting off a chair, she sits down*) So, what are we supposed to do? Shake hands? Hug? This is a little strange for me. I guess I'm not sure how to greet someone whom I've never met. You'll forgive my manners, I'm sure.

JOETTA

Yeah, sure thing. And you'll forgive me my manners, too. I mean, hell, this isn't something I do every day, either. (*getting very nervous*) A hug'd be nice, but I understand if ya don't want to. I'd just like to look atcha for a minute or two. Especially since you're someone who, whom I haven't seen in thirty years, either…but (*trying to make a joke*) by god, I'd have known ya damn near anywhere. Do ya want something to drink? There's a little ice left that the heat hasn't melted yet, and I've got some bourbon, some Coca Cola, a little 7-UP…what's your weakness?

AUDIE

Weakness?

JOETTA

(Trying to keep things light) I mean, what do ya like? I can try to send out for something different if ya want. That guy at the desk, did you meet him? Couldn't find his ass with a compass and two roadmaps, but I'll bet for a couple of bucks, he could scare up something else liquor-wise. You want me to call him? He's gonna find us a better room, too. Any time, he'll be callin' down here to move us. Even I know this isn't a real nice room, but this is where he put me…for now, anyway. (she mixes herself another drink and sits on the edge of the bed) Hey, that's real nice luggage you got there. Musta set you back a dime or two, huh? I had some nice luggage once. Last time I saw it, though, it was in the window of the Drop'n Shop pawn store in Wichita Falls. That was twenty-five years ago. Wonder if it's still there? It was real pretty. It had this green pearl-lookin' finish on the sides, and these brass locks…damn, nothin' I ever put in the suitcases was worth as much as the cases themselves….

AUDIE

(coldly listening to the story) A little bourbon, and a little ice.

JOETTA

What?

A COMFORT BREEZE

AUDIE

I said that I'd like a little bourbon and a little ice if it's not too much trouble. I can get it myself, if you'd like.

JOETTA

(*Rushing to make the drink*)   No..no way, sugar plumb. You sit right there, and let Joetta get it for ya. I can mix a drink faster than a squirrel can screw. (*looking at Audie*)   Oh, I'm sorry. I don't mean to embarrass you. Sometimes I juss talk that way. I don't mean anything by it. It juss comes out. Colorful, that's what I am sometimes, but I don't mean to hurt anyone…hell, down at the beauty parlor, the girls kinda get a kick out of it.

AUDIE

I'll bet they do.

JOETTA

Yeah, they tell me, "Joetta, why don't you tell us some of them, I mean, THOSE stories about life and loves and juss what makes you tick," and I'll get started on stories about growin' up in west Texas, and all of the fun I had, the parties I went to, the boys I knew, well, we laugh and joke around, and before ya know it, the place is cleared out, and I'm the only one left in the shop, except for Pam, that's my hairdresser. I guess they all have somewhere else to be…yep, the rest juss go on home or leave to do errands, or go to meet friends for lunch…but we sure have us a time. There was this one time I was tellin' a story about ol' Ted Belew. If he wasn't the damnedest rounder you ever met. Well, ol' Ted and me was drinkin' beers and laughin', and all of a sudden his wife Penny came stormin' in lookin' for him. She had this charm bracelet with all of this shit hangin on it that clattered like an old pickup truck every time she took a step, and Ted yelled, "Hell, why didn't any of you sons of bitches tell me she was comin'…you know I can't hear her. I'm deaf in one ear." Well, she grabbed him off of that barstool, and *(starts to laugh)* punched him right on his other ear. He sat there for a second or two, got up all bloody and said, "Now, I'll never hear her comin'…she done busted up my GOOD ear." Anyway, she--

AUDIE
Listen, I didn't come here to hear stories about barroom brawls. I didn't drive fifteen hours to have someone like you tell me--

JOETTA
(embarrassed and angry) Someone like me? What's that supposed to mean? What does that mean? I want you to tell me. We haven't even had a, "So, how was your trip? Didja have any car trouble? What didja see along the way." Nothin'. This isn't a real good start, do ya think? I feel some tension here, and we haven't even really started talkin'. This is kinda quick isn't it?

AUDIE
I'm sorry. I didn't mean for it to sound that way. I only meant that….

A COMFORT BREEZE

JOETTA

I know what you meant. When people like you refer to people like me as "someone like you" that means that you look down on me. Right? Am I right? That means--

AUDIE

No, not really. It was a poor choice of words, that's all. I don't even know you. How can I say--

JOETTA

You already did say. Do you want to know how many times I've heard "someone like you" in my life?

AUDIE

I'm sorry. I'm sorry. I want to hear the rest of your story…please.

JOETTA

(looking circumspect) Not now. That story's for my friends. I don't know if you qualify, yet. My friends like me. They like my stories. They like it when I make 'em laugh. I didn't see you laugh once, not once. Are you too stuck up to at least grin a little bit? Are you too damn good to gimme a polite listen? Cuz, I think you are. I think you're too damn good to gimme a polite listen. How do you like that? Do you like that even a little bit? Huh? *(Catching herself before she goes too far)* Look, I'm… sorry. *(laughs)* Must be the damn bourbon talkin'. If I had a dime for every time the bourbon talked for me, I'd be at the Ramada right now, and not at this shit hole. C'mon…can't we just start over? Hell, you can even come through the door again if ya like. *(Smiling at*

Audie and talking sweetly) Please? Pretty please with a big ol' buncha sugar, or grape jelly, or somethin' on it?

AUDIE

(smiling for the first time) OK...ok...sure, let's start over. *(Stands up and offers her hand)* The trip was fine. No car trouble. Nothing interesting along the way, unless you count jackrabbits interesting. Hi, I'm Audilia.

JOETTA

(Smiling and taking her hand) Well, that's better, isn't it? I know, and that's such a beautiful name. I'm Joetta Moss. My god, you're lovely...just a lovely woman.

AUDIE

My friends call me Audie. *(she sits back in the chair)*

JOETTA

(sits down) Can I call you Audie?

AUDIE

Please

JOETTA

Well, now...my friends call me Joetta, or Jo. Ya know, you could call me, I dunno, maybe...

AUDIE

What?

A COMFORT BREEZE

JOETTA
Nothing. Never mind. Not now. Maybe later… We'll talk about it later. So, tell me all about yourself. What do you like to do? Do you have any kids? Is your husband a nice guy? Tell me all about him. *(Not giving her time to answer)* Ya know, I was married once to this bastard who used to hit me with a wallet. *(Laughs)* That's right, a wallet, with some damn Indian chief's head beaded right on it. He'd get a face fulla beer, then get pissed off over one thing or another and pull out this beaded wallet and he'd just work me over. Hell, the worst part of it all was that the damn wallet was always empty. All it had in it was the picture of Jane Russell that came in it when he bought it. What kind of grown man carries a beaded wallet, anyway? And keeps the goddamn store-bought picture in it, too. He'd smack me around, but it really didn't hurt. I got used to it. He was a good lookin' son of a bitch, though. Dumber than a coal bucket, but good lookin'. Had this head fulla black hair, and a chest just like Gordon Scott's.

AUDIE
Who?

JOETTA
Gordon Scott. You know, that guy who played Tarzan in the movies? *(Waiting for some kind of reaction)* Gordon goddamn Scott. Doncha know anything? Doncha see movies? He was only the best-looking thing since James Dean, that's all. So, anyway…His name was Danny Hill…wanted everyone to call him 'King', you know, like king of the hill? and that prick sure could put away the beer. Pretty much the only

excuse he needed to drink was waking up. Yep, haulin his ass outta bed was celebration enough. Drank Pearl. Pearl beer. I though it tasted like a urine specimen, but he liked it, so I drank it, too. What we do for our men, am I right? He just took off one day with some chippie that worked at the Dairy Queen. They told me that he kinda came in, ordered a cherry Coke, and she just took off her apron and drove off with him. Left the cherry Coke right there on the counter. Last I heard, they were in Childress or someplace like that. That was fifteen years ago. Probably got a house fulla kids and a Scottie dog by now. Danny always liked Scottie dogs. I kinda thought they looked like a mukluk, but he liked 'em. He had this picture of some damn Scottie dog on the dresser. He said that it was a movie dog, or some sorta shit. Anyway, he always said that someday, when he was on the sunny side of a dollar, he was gonna get one of those dogs. I'll tell ya, the only thing he ever saw the sunny side of was a fuckin' egg on a plate, nothin' more. (*she looks at Audie*) Oh, damn, I've sure 'nuff done it again, haven't I? I've gotta watch my tongue. I'm so sorry. I really am. (*embarrassed*) Please tell me about yourself. I'm just gonna sit here and listen. I've been takin over the whole conversation, haven't I?

AUDIE
Well, I did want to say that… (*there is a loud noise outside*)

JOETTA
Christ on a crutch, what was that? Sounded like a cannon goin' off. I heard a real cannon go off once, and that's just what it sounded like. It was at a

A COMFORT BREEZE 17

football game. This bone-head I went to high school with, 'ol Johnny Price thought it'd be a good idea to set off a cannon whenever the Lions made a touchdown. Well, no one of ever heard the damn thing because the Lions never scored a single point. Never. They'd get all suited up, run around on the field and get a big 'ol ass-kickin every Friday night. Yea...the joke among the girls was, why is it safe to go out with a Lion? Cuz he can't score on ya. *(starts to laugh which turns into a coughing fit)* Well, anyway, the one time, the one and only time we heard the cannon was after the water boy, and I can't even remember his name...a little bitty 'ol kid, didn't get off the field in time, and this big 'ol guy from the other team just mowed him down, just flattened his ass. Well sir, this kid got up, turned around to the crowd and yelled, "Now, THAT'S what Texas football's all about!" The crowd just went crazy. They laughed and cheered, and just about crapped in their pants. I'll tell ya, those were some good times. Some really good times for sure. *(She's still laughing)*

AUDIE
Can I say something?

JOETTA
Well, sure you can, honey. Just jump right in any 'ol time.

AUDIE
I'm trying, really trying to be nice, to listen to your stories, and figure out just who you are. All you've been doing is dominating the conversation with reminiscences of the old days, and skirting around the

reason that I'm here. Do you understand? I'm trying to be kind here. And, I don't want to hurt you, but I didn't come this far to take trips down memory lane with you. I think you owe me more than that. Don't you?

JOETTA

See, you're doing it again…you're going too fast, and I'm not too sure that I understand. I just thought that maybe—

AUDIE

No, you understand.

JOETTA

(*after a long silence*) I don't want to get into that right now. Please, just let me ease into it, can't you? Just give me my time. I just don't believe in just jumping in. Every time in my life that I jumped in to anything, I got screwed. Literally, and every other way, screwed.

AUDIE

I'm not out to screw you, as you say. I just need to know. Who am I? Who are you? What in the hell am I doing here, and how long before you tell me something?

JOETTA

(*crying silently, and after a pause*) You're my daughter, you know that. My goddamn child. Is that what you want to hear? You already know. Can't you just let me explain in my own way? Do you think this is easy for me? This isn't at all the way it was spoze to work out. I wanted us to be friends before I told you things, maybe have some drinks, maybe go out and eat, or something.

AUDIE
Friends! I don't even know you. All I know, so far, is a cheap motel room, some bad liquor, and stories of west Texas. What am I supposed to go back with, this and a postcard? Am I supposed to go back home and say that I met my mother, and she knows some guy who used to shoot off a cannon at ball games? She got hit with a wallet by someone who looked like Gordon "somebody"?

JOETTA
(Bluntly) Scott. Gordon Scott!

AUDIE
Gordon Scott. Is that all there is about you? My god, you're how old? Forty-five, fifty? Oh, and you had nice luggage at one time, and it's in some damn pawn shop. Oh, yeah, that's a lot to take back. Well, I'm sorry…that's not enough. Not nearly enough. You owe me everything that you can tell me. You can tell me now, or you can tell later, but you're going to talk to me. Do you understand?

JOETTA
He didn't look like Gordon Scott. I said that his chest looked like Gordon Scott's.

AUDIE
(Angrily) You're still not listening. Who gives one big damn about his chest? Is this part of the "Joetta"

tapestry? Is this what you're trying to get across to me? Goddammit, I've spent my whole life with everyone I know skirting around things, and I'm sure as hell not going to come this far to have you do it, too. Don't let the looks fool you. Don't be overly impressed with the suitcase, and the clothes. Don't let the--

JOETTA

What? What? Don't be impressed with what? I shouldn't like to see someone that I got rid of doing well? I shouldn't like the fact that someone I've thought about twenty times a day for all these years is a success? Don't give me that working-man's ethic crap. You don't look like you've missed out on too much in life. Not like me. You know who I went to parties with? Anyone with two bucks and a rubber in his wallet, that's who! And, most of the time is was after the parties...that's right...after the parties. Those boys would get all hot and worked up with their 'real' girlfriends, and when the girls wouldn't come across, they'd call 'ol Joetta up, and off we'd go. I knew exactly what the back seat of every high school boy's car looked like, cuz I was in every one of 'em. And, more than once, too. Hell, if I hadn't let those boys do what they wanted to do with me, I wouldn't have had any dates at all. I was the one that no one wanted to take out during the day. Do you know what that's like? Do you? If some boy talked to me in the hall at school, I'd see the 'looks' from everyone. I'd hear the laughs behind my back.

AUDIE

Don't do this…

A COMFORT BREEZE

JOETTA

Don't do what? Don't tell you about myself? Don't tell you that your mother was the town punch? I thought that's what you wanted to hear about. Don't tell you that anyone who was nice to me got it on the first date? Date...hell, that's a nice way to say 'pick up'. (*pauses*) See, that's all I was. Don't you understand? For years, I prayed that some new guy would move to town, and for a day or two, maybe...maybe, he wouldn't find out what I was like, that the other kids in school wouldn't tell him about me...that I could be asked out before midnight like the other girls. (*starts to cry*) All alone, late in the night, I'd hold my pillow, and pretend that I was anywhere else, and that no one knew that Joetta Moss was the easy girl in town, the one that couldn't remember if it was Robert, Bill, Troy or David that had screwed her the weekend before. All I wanted was to get to know someone before it happened, ya know? Was that too much to ask? So, don't come in here with your fancy clothes and tell me how hard you had it. No one who looks like you had it that bad. You didn't dread the mornings like I did. I dreaded the mornings because in the mornings, real life started all over again. (*She's crying silently*)

AUDIE

You might be surprised, Joetta. You might be surprised that--

JOETTA

(*Shocked*) My god...you used my name. (*she stops crying*) You used my damn name! That's nice. Really nice. I kinda like that. You lovely, beautiful woman.

Oh, my god...I hate myself for telling you those things. It was cruel. I guess deep down, I wanted you to think that you came from 'something'. You know what I mean. I didn't want you to think that I was...well, what I am. That's a bad way to put it, but you know what I mean, doncha? That I'm--

AUDIE
I know what you mean. And, it was a perfectly good way to put it. I guess that I...

JOETTA
Knew? Knew what I might be like? I'm so sorry, child. It takes an effort to 'be someone', and all my life, I wanted to 'be someone'. I didn't wanna be famous in Eagle Flats, Texas for...well, what I was famous for...

AUDIE
I know. *(smiles)* What is it they say? That if you had the same number of penises sticking out of you that you've had stuck in you, you'd look like a porcupine? *(they both look at each other, pause, then begin to laugh)*

JOETTA
(laughing really hard) Well, by damn, you're right! That's a good one. You DO have a sense of humor...now, that's funny...porcupine. Well, hell, I guess that's what I WOULD look like, I never thought of it that way. It sorta sets up this crazy picture in my head, but I get it. *(both are still laughing)* Hey, I've got one for ya. This guy calls into work and tells his boss, "I can't come in to work today. I'm really sick."

A COMFORT BREEZE 23

And, the boss says, "So, how sick are ya?" and the guy says, "Well, I'm screwing my five year old daughter." (*Audie stops laughing, but Joetta doesn't notice*) Now, that a good one *(she's still laughing)*. 'Ol Butch Pattison told me that one. Now, he was a rounder, too. One time, he was on this Cushman Eagle scooter, and he...*(notices Audie)* What's the matter? Didn't you think that was funny? See, this guy calls his boss, and--

AUDIE
I got it. I got the joke.

JOETTA
You didn't think it was even a little bit funny? See, I thought after what you said about the porcupines that-

AUDIE
No, that's not it. It wasn't the joke.

JOETTA
I thought maybe it was. I mean, we were laughing and talking and, well...I know it wasn't exactly the most tasteful joke of all time, but I thought that it was kinda funny. See, when Butch told me that one, we were out in front of the drugstore, and--

AUDIE
Please, just PLEASE, don't go into another story. Not right now. Let's just talk about something else, can we?

JOETTA
But why? Did I say something wrong? You don't somehow know Butch do you? You don't have something against him, do you? Cuz, I always thought he was kinda no-count, but damn funny. Is that it? You knew him from somewhere?

AUDIE
Look, I have no idea who Butch is, and I don't really care who Butch is. I guess the joke just hit a little close to home, that's all. Hasn't anything ever, you know, hit close to home with you?

JOETTA
Oh, I get it. You had a bad boss at one time. You knew some boss who caused you some trouble, is that it?

AUDIE
(*quietly*) Yes, that's it. Sure, a bad boss. A really bad boss.

JOETTA
Well, tell me about him. Maybe that'll make it all better. Sometimes when I talk about stuff, I feel all better. And, I could write books about bad bosses. One time, I worked for this silly son of a bitch who used to stuff a big 'ol buncha napkins in his pants, and tell all of the girls, "Made ya look, didn't I?" It was at the old Chicken Plate restaurant. Not the new Chicken Plate that they built after the tornado blew the old one down. Funny, after they opened the new place, no one ever came anymore. Same cook, same menu, hell, same silverware, but no one came. We just stood there

night after night, and no one showed up. The place finally closed. I think it's an insurance office, now. That was out in Herford. I think it's because we moved out on the highway instead of stayin' downtown, but I dunno... Maybe everyone just got tired of chicken.

AUDIE

That's got to be it. (*she smiles*) Chicken can get a little old, I guess.

JOETTA

Oh, honey...we had chicken, and Mexican food, and pork chops. We had everything you can imagine. And, the best fried potatoes in Texas, just the BEST. The owner, he wasn't the one with the napkins, he just couldn't make it work. He changed up the decorations to look like this cantina sorta deal. Before, it just looked like...I dunno, this regular café. You know what I mean? Nothin' special. Just a place to eat. I guess he just went too high-dollar, and made it look all fancy-like. People out there don't want fancy. They just want food, and the more grease it's floatin' in, the better they like it. I'll tell ya something, if your chili wasn't sittin three inches under that orange film, it wasn't fit to eat. Now, that's the truth. Best chili I ever ate, though...ever, anywhere. We had this 'ol wetback named Ernesto who'd been in town for about thirty years, he was the cook. This guy could make anything ya wanted, and, I swear, people came for miles to eat his food. Everyone in town knew he was just illegal as hell, but no one reported him because they didn't wanna miss out on his cookin'. After the place closed up, Ernesto just took off. No one ever did know what happened to him. He sure was a good 'ol boy, though. I'll tell ya, more than once he'd toss me a kitchen towel because I was cryin' over one thing or another. He just kinda knew when folks were in trouble, ya know? He'd always tell me, (*doing a bad Mexican accent*) "Eees okay, missy…it be all better in some days later." And, he was right. In some days later, things were all better. I sure miss him, ya know, sometimes…

AUDIE
Me, too.

JOETTA
What d'ya mean? What d'ya mean "me, too?"

AUDIE
I had those days, too…when "it be all better in some days later."

JOETTA
You have some things to tell me, doncha?

AUDIE
Yes, I guess I do. I mean, I know I do. I'm just not ready quite yet. I'm too private sometimes. I've always been too private, I guess.

JOETTA
Well, you have questions. Don't you think I have questions? I saw you for ten minutes thirty years ago, and that's it. I have questions, too. Thirty years worth of questions.

A COMFORT BREEZE 27

AUDIE

What did you see? Please talk me.

JOETTA

What?

AUDIE

Tell me... tell me what you saw thirty years ago for ten minutes. I want to know.

JOETTA

(*after a long pause*) Well, I saw...Look, this isn't easy for me. I want you to know that. (*going to mix another drink and lighting a cigarette. After another long pause*) Well... Oh, god, here we go. I saw (*Joetta can't look at her*) This isn't going to make any sense at all. It's just gonna sound, I dunno...I saw the face of God. That sounds silly, doesn't it? I saw the most beautiful thing ever created layin' there all wet, and cryin', and wrapped up in this little pink blanket. I saw these tiny fingers reaching out for someone to take hold of 'em. (*starts to cry silently*) I saw this face that had her whole life ahead of her, and I saw this little red spot right in the middle of your forehead, and I was sure, just sure that...well, that was the place where God had put his finger on you, to make everything good for you. You had this little crooked smile, even while you were crying, and it was the smile of the angels. (*she laughs a little*) Oh...and, you were a tough little thing, too. You looked like you were trying to say that nothing and no one were ever gonna stop you. You looked like, "Gimme fifteen minutes, and I'll be ready to take on the world." (*she *turns and smiles at Audie)* You looked like you had every secret of life in you, and couldn't wait to tell the world about it. I just looked at you and cried, and cried some more. I couldn't stop. That was the happiest day of my life, and it was the saddest day of my life, both at the same time. Both rolled up into one… both… just… anyway…See, I wanted to buy clothes for you, and show you off, and tell the world to look at you because you were mine. I wanted to laugh with you, and take you on trips, and warn you about anything bad in life. I wanted to see you in your first Halloween costume, and I wanted to make you your first birthday cake for you. I wanted to… to…(*she is sobbing by now*) I wanted you to call me… "Mom"….I just wanted to hear that ONE time. Mom. Was that too much to ask? You were the first thing that was really mine, and no one else's. I saw in you all of the things that…that…I wanted, and…God, help me! Please God, help me through this! (*screams*) God, you son of a bitch! I can't do this! Why? Why? This isn't spoze to be like this! It's spoze to….What did I do? I was wrong. So wrong! Did you hear me? I called God a son of a bitch. I…I...Oh, God help me….Please somebody help me! Just….

AUDIE

(*shocked, and going to her*) It's okay. It really is okay. We don't have to do this now. We can talk about something else. (*puts her arm on Joetta's shoulder*) Tell me a story. Tell me one of those "Joetta west Texas" stories. Please….tell me about Butch, or the Chicken Plate restaurant, or… I know. Tell me all about that luggage you used to have. Tell me all about that. It was green, wasn't it? And, it had

A COMFORT BREEZE 29

brass locks, and what else? What else was there about it? Hey, you know what? Listen to me…listen. I had a beaded wallet one time. *(Joetta, still crying begins to listen)* I did. A beaded wallet. It had Dale Evans on it, but the beading was really crappy, and it looked like Dale was winking all the time. *(Joetta smiles)* It looked like this *(Audie exaggerating the wink)*. I called it my lucky wallet because there was always someone winking at me. *(Joetta laughs a little)* And, you know how I got it? I swiped it from Woolworth's. That's right. And, I felt really bad about it, but I didn't return it. I'd been looking at it for weeks, and one day, I just walked out with it in my hand. No one even noticed. That's the only thing I ever took from a store without paying for it. At least the only thing I can remember. Oh, and Dale had this bright red hair, too. She kind of looked more like a circus clown than the real Dale Evans, but I knew it was her, so that's all that mattered. I loved that wallet. I think it was always my favorite, and probably still is. It had this zipper pocket in it for change, and a bright red string on the side. Now, isn't that silly? After all these years, that's the wallet I remember most fondly. Now, why would I think about that? Why now? So, see? You're not the only one who's led an interesting life. You're trapped in a motel room with a genuine thief. *(she laughs as does Joetta)* Hey, maybe they'll make one of those gangster movies about me. What do you think? Huh? A gangster movie? Since Bonnie Parker is dead, I guess I'll have to play myself. *(they both laugh)* Outside of her, I guess I'm the only one mean enough to pull it off. Do you think?

JOETTA
(*trying to compose herself, but still upset*) I guess we're a real pair, aren't we? You come in here lookin' like you just stepped out of Look Magazine, and then there's me…lookin' like I just stepped out of an '81 Bellaire, and ya know why? Cuz I just stepped out of an '81 Bellaire, that's why. I'll tell ya somethin' though. It's the best runnin' damn car I've had in my life. Hey, what kinda car do you have, a Cadillac, a Lincoln, what?

AUDIE
(*Surprised that Joetta's mood could change so quickly*) That doesn't really matter.

JOETTA
No, tell me…what kind? Some foreign deal, am I right? Some foreign deal?

AUDIE
No one cares.

JOETTA
Oh, c'mon…tell me. What kind?

AUDIE
A Rolls.

JOETTA
A "Rolls." What's that? What's a Rolls? What kinda car is that?

AUDIE
A Rolls Royce, but it's--

A COMFORT BREEZE 31

JOETTA

Sleepin' Jesus! A Rolls Royce? How much did THAT set you back? A lot? I mean, was it a whole lot? Damn, I've never even seen a Rolls Royce, much less ridden in one. The most expensive car I ever got in was Bud Tuttle's grandmother's Buick, and that was just to smell it cuz it was new. But, a Rolls Royce.

AUDIE

It's a lease.

JOETTA

(Not understanding) "Aleese"? That's a girl's name. Is that the model, or something?

AUDIE

No, a LEASE. That means I just rent it. I don't really own it.

JOETTA

Well, who's the dumb son of a bitch who'd rent out a car like that?

AUDIE

Are you all right? It's just that one minute you were so very upset, and now you seem--

JOETTA

I'm okay. I can do that. I know it seems a little strange, but my mother used to tell me that I'd always be better in a minute, and she was right. She'd get this old clock out and say, "See this big hand? When it get here, you'll feel all better." And, she was right. Now, whenever I'm upset, I imagine that clock in my head, and I can make myself feel better. It's just tricking myself, but it always works.

AUDIE
It's just that I've never seen anyone able to recover so fast from being that upset. Are you sure? Are you sure you're all right?

JOETTA
The only thing I wasn't able to use that clock on was when I had to say goodbye to you. That was the toughest one. I imagined every kind of clock there was, and it still didn't help, not one little bit. I saw clocks for three years after that. After we had to say "goodbye."

AUDIE
I use birds.

JOETTA
What?

AUDIE
Birds. I use birds. I tell myself that by the time that bird flies away, everything will be better. I've done that all of my life.

JOETTA
I guess that could work, too. Birds. I'd have never thought of that. You drive a Rolls Royce, and YOU, of all people hafta think past your problems? See, I'd have thought that—

A COMFORT BREEZE

AUDIE
It's not the car. It's never the car. Don't you see what I'm trying to tell you? Everyone has problems. We all have problems. I just don't let mine show. I just keep-

JOETTA
But, you drive a--

AUDIE
(*angrily*) Don't say it! Don't say the name of that damn car again. I don't want to hear that from you anymore. Do you understand? My life doesn't revolve around some obscenely expensive car.

JOETTA
I think it does.

AUDIE
What's that supposed to mean?

JOETTA
I think your life does revolve around your car, and your luggage, and your clothes, and--

AUDIE
Stop it. Just stop it! I don't have to listen to you. This has gone on far too long. Just leave me alone about it, will you? (*both sit silently, awkwardly for many seconds*)

JOETTA
So, you're telling me that you do or DON'T wanna talk about your car? (*both look at each other then start to laugh*)

AUDIE
I DON'T want to talk about it. (*still laughing*) Damn.

JOETTA
Cuz, I'm right here.

AUDIE
You've got tenacity, I'll give you that.

JOETTA
I think it was Dean Collier that gave me "tenacity" one time, but the doctor cured it with penicillin. (*both laugh*)

AUDIE
My god, that's awful.

JOETTA
No, I'm telling you the truth. Dean and I were--

AUDIE
Not that…the joke.

JOETTA
I know. I know what that means. But I did catch something from Dean that wasn't real pretty. Hell, his uncle was a doctor, too. You'd have thought that he'd a been a little, I dunno, a little…

AUDIE
Cleaner?

A COMFORT BREEZE

JOETTA
Naw. Better in bed. (*both laugh at her joke*) Dean played the guitar, and...

AUDIE
Lots of people play the guitar.

JOETTA
Not like Dean. He could make ya cry with that thing. He was self-taught, too. There wasn't anything that he couldn't play. At lunch, during school, he'd get that guitar out of the trunk of his car, and he'd go to town on it. The kids would call out a song, and Dean would take off on it. One day, he just quit. He traded the guitar in on a set of old beat-up drums, and he--

AUDIE
Was great at the drums, too?

JOETTA
Oh, hell no. He was awful. Sounded like he was beatin' on an old car fender. I'm sorry. I said "car" didn't I? (*she laughs*) He was always gonna join a rock and roll band. Last I heard, he was workin' right there at the tire store in Eagle Flats, replacin' valve stems, or somethin' like that. Never did get that rock and roll job. Lost dreams, I spoze. That happened to a lot of the kids I knew. Most of 'em, in fact.

AUDIE
How about a drink?

JOETTA
I already have one.

AUDIE
No, me. I'd like a drink. (*goes to mix something*) There's no more ice left.

JOETTA
I'll call that guy at the desk, again. (*picks up phone*) Hey, this is Joetta, again. I know you don't have another room, yet. No, we need some more ice. I know there's a machine. How 'bout you bring it down? What d'ya mean, "busy"? You're on your ass watchin' TV. Cuz, I know you are. Okay…Okay…No, I'll get it. Well, cuz I wouldn't want you to hafta miss your shows. Well, ya might learn somethin', and that'd put you right up there in the genius category. Sure, it would. Okay, that's fine. *(Hangs up)* Lissin, I'm gonna get some more ice. D'ya wanna come with me?

AUDIE
No, I'll just wait here.

JOETTA
That's fine, sugar. I'll be right back. (*she takes the ice bucket and leaves*) Can I get you anything?

AUDIE
No, I'm okay. Thank you, though.

> *Joetta exits. This gives Audie time to look through Joetta's things, the razor, her suitcase…she looks as if to try to figure out who Joetta is. She is careful to place everything back just as she's found it. As she looks, Audie is very*

A COMFORT BREEZE

> *thoughtful as to what everything means. She looks at her clothes, her make-up, and even her underwear. This should not be "thrown away." Audie should give each item careful consideration. This is almost a pantomime, and not to be rushed. She hears Joetta returning, and quickly closes the suitcase.*

AUDIE

Well, did you get it? Did you have any trouble?

JOETTA

Naw, not at all. I was right, though. That guy at the desk was on his ass, TV blarin' away, and a newspaper was over his face. He was sound asleep. Why couldn't I ever get a job like that? Just sit around all day and screw off work. Oh, and there was a hole in the sole of his shoe. I could see him right through the window. And, guess what! I saw your car and there's a big 'ol scratch right on the door.

AUDIE

(looking out the door) Really? Where? I don't see it!

JOETTA

I'm lyin' to ya. *(laughs)* I thought you didn't care about that car?

AUDIE

(Smiles) Don't start. Just please, don't start that again. *(She gets ice and mixes a drink)*

JOETTA
I've got it. Let's play a game.

AUDIE
Oh, please. Are you serious?

JOETTA
Sure, I'm serious. C'mon.

AUDIE
I'd feel kind of silly playing a game. That's not really why I came here. What kind of game? I mean…

JOETTA
Oh, I dunno…how 'bout 'guess the person'? C'mon, it'll be fun. Just try it, okay?

AUDIE
Guess the person? How do you play that? What's "guess the person?"

JOETTA
I'll think of a person, and you have ten questions to find about who it is. All I can answer is "yes" or "no." Then, it's your turn to think of someone. Wanna play? I've gotta get a drink first, though. (*she mixes a drink*)

AUDIE
I don't know. I really don't play games, and…(*sees that Joetta really wants this*) Okay, sure. I'll try it. I'd rather not, but…

JOETTA
(*sits on the bed*) Okay, I've got someone….

A COMFORT BREEZE

AUDIE
So, what do I do, again?

JOETTA
So, you start askin' questions.

AUDIE
Sure. All right. Is it a man?

JOETTA
Oh, hell yes!

AUDIE
Is he living?

JOETTA
Unfortunately. Okay, I'm sorry. Yes.

AUDIE
Is he famous?

JOETTA
Does a police blotter count?

AUDIE
No. I don't think so.

JOETTA
Then, no. He's not famous. Well…No. No, he's not.

AUDIE
Do you know him personally?

JOETTA
Same answer. "Unfortunately."

AUDIE
How many questions is that?

JOETTA
I dunno, four or five. Keep askin'…C'mon.

AUDIE
Does he look like someone else?

JOETTA
Part of him does.

AUDIE
I know. I know who it is. It's that guy who had the beaded wallet and he looked like Gordon "what's his name".

JOETTA
That's right! It's Danny! And, it's Scott…Gordon SCOTT! And, it was his CHEST, his CHEST that looked like Gordon Scott's. He didn't look like him. Just his chest. Come to think of it, Danny didn't look like anyone. Just Danny. It's sad, too because he always wanted to look like Kirk Douglas. He would even stick himself in the chin with a pencil to get that dimple. You know, that 'thing' Kirk has in his chin? That hole?

AUDIE
(Laughs) Kirk Douglas? Did it work?

A COMFORT BREEZE

JOETTA
Hell, no. All he looked like was some idiot with pencil lead in his chin.

AUDIE
Was he the "one"...was he "Mister Right" for you, even with all of the bad stuff? I just wondered because--

JOETTA
Oh, noooo...not at all. Not even in the ballpark. He was just someone to pass the time with. I didn't really even have to marry him. It just seemed like the thing to do, I guess. He made me laugh at a time when I needed to laugh. Do you know what I mean? I just needed a laugh or two. I was coming out of a bad situation...one more of many, and...(*stops herself*) Let's not talk about this right now. It's your turn. Think of someone.

AUDIE
I don't want to play right now. I'd rather...

JOETTA
You've got to play right now. It's your turn. There are only two of us here. I can't very well skip you, and come back later. Now, think of someone. I'll give you five seconds. Ready? Go. (*she looks at her watch*)

AUDIE
Okay, okay...I've got someone. Do I have to play right now?

JOETTA
You're playin'…that's it. Is it a man?

AUDIE
Maybe.

JOETTA
Now, wait a minute. It's either a man, or it's not. Is it a woman?

AUDIE
I don't know.

JOETTA
Please. You're not doin' this right. Damn. Is it a dog or somethin'?

AUDIE
I'm not sure.

JOETTA
Look, I've wasted three questions, and you don't even know what it is? Is it real?

AUDIE
No. It's not real. Not at all.

JOETTA
Then, it's like a cartoon? Is that it? A cartoon character?

AUDIE
I guess so. That's as close as I've ever figured out.

A COMFORT BREEZE

JOETTA
(*getting frustrated*) Okay…it's not a man, it's not a woman, it's not a dog, but it's like a cartoon, but maybe not? And, it's not real? That doesn't make any sense.

AUDIE
I told you that I didn't want to play right now.

JOETTA
Then I give up. I'm usually pretty good at this, too. So, who is it?

AUDIE
I just don't want to say, please.

JOETTA
Look, it's just a silly-ass game. So, tell me. Who is it? Or, what is it?

AUDIE
It's God, okay? God. I thought that would be a good one. And, besides…

JOETTA
Hold on. Wait a minute. You're saying that God's not real? Is that what you're telling me, that you don't believe in God? Hell, EVERYONE believes in God. What's wrong with you?

AUDIE
You believe in God? After all that's happened to—

JOETTA
Hell, yes, I believe in God.

AUDIE
Why? Why do you believe? Just tell me.

JOETTA
Well, because. I mean, I believe in God, that's all… because he…well, because I just do, okay?

AUDIE
Because of the wonderful life you've had? Because you've been so happy, and good things have come to you?

JOETTA
No, not that. Not because of that. I just think that…well, you're s'posed to. That's it. And, if you believe hard enough, then something good's gonna come along, someday.

AUDIE
Let me ask you something, and I want you to be really honest with me.

JOETTA
All right.

AUDIE
Is it that you're afraid not to…not to believe in God? Is that it?

A COMFORT BREEZE

JOETTA
Well, they do say "God fearin'" don't they? Aren't you spoze to be a little bit scared? I guess I'm scared that I might screw up and make him mad. (*long pause*) But, I screw up a lot. Maybe I'm a little late for that. I guess if God can still like me, he can like anyone.

AUDIE
I'm sorry. I didn't mean to make you feel badly. It's just that God, or whatever it is never spent much time helping me, that's all.

JOETTA
Well, didja ever ask? Ever really ask for help?

AUDIE
Every day of my life until I was about twelve, that's all. Every goddamn day, and you know what? Nothing happened. When I was twelve, I remember I was eating a biscuit, and I went out in a rainstorm and stood by the clothesline. And, I begged God to kill me. Begged him! And, you know what happened? Nothing. Not one damn thing. All that happened was that I got whipped for being out in the rain and eating a biscuit between meals. After that, I knew that God wasn't real, and that I was completely on my own.

JOETTA
That's a terrible thing for you to do. What if something had happened? What if you'd been hurt? What if—

AUDIE
But, don't you see? I was hurt. I was hurt by a black leather belt, and the bastard who hit me with it. And, kept hitting me until…until I did what was necessary to make it stop. I was always doing what was necessary to make it stop. Anything to make it…

JOETTA
(*almost speechless*) Oh, my god. You poor child. You poor little child. Was it your father? Did he do that to you?

AUDIE
(*after a pause*) My fathers, my uncles, my brothers, my cousins…my… I'm sorry. My life is dictated by plurals, I guess. Multiples of people who did things to me, to…*(she starts to cry in a very controlled way)* I told you I didn't want to play "guess the person" right now. Can I just sit quietly for a minute?

JOETTA
But, I thought that…

AUDIE
PLEASE. I just want to be quiet for a second or two. Please. Please honor that. I'll be all right. Just give me a minute.

JOETTA
I spoze "guess the person" wasn't a good idea, was it? I just thought that it might be a fun way to pass the time. Kinda be an ice-breaker. I didn't mean for it to turn into this. If I knew it'd hurt you, I'd have…

A COMFORT BREEZE

AUDIE
It's all right. I'm just…I guess it's the drink. I really don't drink. Maybe an occasional sherry, but I usually just nurse those along.

JOETTA
Well, I don't exactly nurse 'em along. I usually slam 'em down, and that's not good. I know it, but my god, I do love the grape, as they say. I can do without the hangovers, but the lead-up is a hell of a lot of fun. I knew this guy once who could drink a whole beer at once. Just pour it right down his gullet in one swallow. Damnedest thing you ever saw. People would keep buyin' 'em for him, and he'd just keep pourin' 'em down. Have you ever seen anything like that?

AUDIE
(*recovering*) Not really, but I saw a woman paint a picture of Richard Nixon with garden gloves.

JOETTA
Ya mean Nixon was wearing garden gloves in the picture?

AUDIE
No, no. The woman dipped the gloves in paint then she splashed paint on a huge canvas. After she was through, it was Nixon.

JOETTA
Well, damn. Where was that?

AUDIE

In New Orleans. Have you ever been there?

JOETTA

Once, a long time ago. It's a fun town, that's for sure. Hey, do they still sell those hotdogs from those street carts? Those were the best damn things I ever ate. I think they were a quarter back then. I'm sure they cost more now.

AUDIE

Yes, I'm sure they do. I've never had one, though. Listen, do you want to know something? We've been here for a long time. We've had drinks, we've played games, we've talked about everything except what I came here for and, what you've been wanting to know about me. I love your stories. I really do, but we could have done this visit over a phone. I'm going to ask you nicely, with a big 'ol buncha sugar, or grape jelly on it, to please tell me what I'm doing here. I have to know.

JOETTA

(*ignoring her*) Ya know, I knew this girl in school who could do anything. She could sing, dance, do all kinds of stuff. There wasn't anything she couldn't do. Ya know what she did for art class one time?

AUDIE

Please, not now…

JOETTA

She carved this little horse out a block of wood. That's right, just got this block of wood and carved a

A COMFORT BREEZE

horse out of it. It was perfect, really nice, and it was running, too. This running horse, and--

AUDIE

Not now, Joetta!

JOETTA

I think she's probably famous by now. One of those that anything she did, she was gonna be famous for, ya know what I mean? She won all kinds of prizes for her stuff. She was even home-comin' queen one year. The boys were... well really, everyone was just crazy about her. Ya know... she was the first person I ever knew who went skinny dippin'. Anyway, her name was--

AUDIE

Dammit, PLEASE!

JOETTA

The rest of us had this crap made outta paper, and popcycle sticks, but not her. She--

AUDIE

Goddammit, enough! That's enough. I don't care what you did in art class, *(starts for the door)* I'm leaving. I'm leaving this room right now, if you don't start talking to me. I'm not playing with you. Not anymore.

JOETTA

(The curtains start to move in the dingy room) Ya feel that?

AUDIE
What?

JOETTA
That little breeze comin' up. That's a real west Texas comfort breeze, that is.

AUDIE
It's just a wind, that's all. Just a small wind.

JOETTA
(Feeling the liquor a little more) That's where you're wrong. Hell, there were times when that was the only thing between nekkid and dyin' in the old days. When we were kids, we'd pray for a comfort breeze. Goddamn, this heat is swelterin.' Are you hot?

AUDIE
(Firmly) Tell me. You tell me what I came to hear. I don't want to listen to a weather report. You owe me more than that.

JOETTA
(after a long pause) I first met your daddy when I was in the third grade. Hell, I was all decked out in a blue dress and about three petticoats, I think…maybe it was four. I don't remember for sure. Anyway, he came into the classroom, and he was the most beautiful thing I'd ever seen. He'd just moved to Eagle Flats from Lovington, New Mexico.

AUDIE
I don't want hear this, not more filler stories. I want to hear--

A COMFORT BREEZE

JOETTA
(*getting angry*) Lissin'…you're gonna hear it all, or you can just get back in that goddamn car and head right outta here. You think I like this? You think I like givin' my whole life out to you? I don't even know you. You come boppin' in here with your fancy clothes and your wallet fulla credit cards, and your fancy luggage. Who are you? And, just who in the hell do you THINK you are, anyway? Are you better than me? ARE YOU? Well, tell me! (*There is a long silence. Audie looks away. She knows that this is what Joetta hasn't wanted to tell her*) Look, I'm sorry, I'm sorry as I can be, I just…I…(*quietly*) He was the most beautiful boy, your daddy. He became a beautiful man, too.

AUDIE
Do you want another drink?

JOETTA
I may do that. I just may do that. (*she mixes another drink*) I loved that son of a bitch from the first time I saw him. He was tall, and he was wearing this blue jean jacket with these little western studs all over it. There was no better lookin' third grader that God ever made…that's all. And, when he smiled, we all just about died.

AUDIE
Go on, please.

JOETTA
Every girl in school wanted to sit by him, and every boy wanted to be his best friend. He was golden…just

golden. He was the most golden thing ever created. *(She begins to cry quietly)*

AUDIE

What was his name? Please tell me his name. You haven't told me his name, and I have a right to know.

JOETTA

(*after a long pause*) Robert. It was Robert…Rutlege. Everyone called him Lacy, though. (*quietly*) Lacy…

AUDIE

Are you all right? If not, we can—

JOETTA

(Wiping tears away) Lacy had money, too. Hell, before the Rutleges moved to town, the only one with two nickels to rub together was 'ol Spencer Dick, the pharmacist. Hey, ya wanna hear somethin' funny? (*smiling*) His wife's name was Hatta *(starts to laugh out loud)*. Now, can you imagine goin' through life bein' called Hatta Dick? (*both are laughing now*) She…she…(*laughing really hard*) she tried to get everyone to call her Lanette, that was her middle name, but no one ever did. She went all over Eagle Flats tellin' folks to call her Lanette, and they'd say, "sure thing, Mrs. Dick," and then they'd laugh behind her back. Oh, that poor woman. I don't think she ever signed a check that someone wouldn't chuckle a little.

AUDIE

(Still laughing) Can I have another drink, too?

A COMFORT BREEZE 53

JOETTA

Sure thing. Help yourself. Anyway, your daddy and I got hooked up about our junior high school age, off and on. Oh, I knew what he was. I knew he was screwin' anything that'd stand still, and a few who wouldn't stand still. But, it didn't matter. Ya know, I don't think he ever passed a test or turned in any homework in school. Not that I recall. He'd just charm the grades right outta those teachers. Women teachers, men teachers…it didn't matter. I told you he was golden, didn't I? Straight A's for nothin' more than smilin' just right.

AUDIE

How did it happen?

JOETTA

What? How did what happen?

AUDIE

How did you get pregnant?

JOETTA

Well, honey…how does anybody get pregnant?

AUDIE

(Looks and nods for an answer)

JOETTA

(Mixing another drink and sits in chair) In the back seat of your daddy's fifty-eight Impala, that's how. After we broke up in junior high because of all of the other girls, well…that's when I started doin' what he was doin'. I wanted to get back at him, I guess.

Funny…if it's a guy, he's a stud. For a girl to do the same thing, well, she's a slut. Anyway, he called me up, and we were at the drive-in movie watchin' "The Day The Earth Stood Still", and it stood still, okay. It stood still for one of us. *(Pauses)* Hey, look, I'm sorry. I'm not makin' fun of it, and I can't make a fuss about it, either. *(Quietly)* It was everything I wanted from him, everything. I knew exactly what I was doin' but this time it was for true love. Not like the other times with the other boys. Whatever means more than love, that's what I felt for him, and that's what it was. Love just wasn't a big enough word. It never was a big enough word. If I live to be a hundred, it still won't be big enough…just…just…

AUDIE
(*quietly*) Then what happened?

JOETTA
(*after a long pause*) You know what he said to me when I finally told him? He just told me to ride a bicycle over a bumpy road or fall down a flight of stairs. Then he… then… he… laughed at me. Sometimes, I can still hear that at night. That laugh. I was sixteen, and I loved him like there was no one else in the world. For ten years, I loved him that much. (*crying quietly*) No one should be cursed to love someone that much. It's not fair.

AUDIE
I know.

A COMFORT BREEZE

JOETTA

No you don't. No one knows….and you know what? With every ounce of love, a pound of hurt came right along with it. You know what I did? I went to the water tower and climbed up the goddamn thing ready to throw myself off. I was gonna show him. Instead… I just sat there and cried. I cried 'till there weren't any more tears. Do you know how long you hafta cry 'til there aren't any more tears? I'll tell you somethin'…to this day, every town I come to, the first thing I do is look for the water tower. Just in case…just in case I might need it.

AUDIE

I'm sorry, I didn't know. I never knew…

JOETTA

No, you never knew, no one ever knew. Do you know what happened to girls who weren't married and got pregnant in 1963? Do you know what Eagle Flats, Texas was like back then? It's not like it is now…girls havin' babies, no repercussions. See, I know some big words, too. Hell, they even give 'em showers now days. Back then it was different. I remember there was this guy who was caught peepin' in windows back in high school. He was fifteen. He and his whole damn family were run outta town. I was pregnant, for god's sake. A town of eleven thousand people and every one of 'em with a Bible in their pocket, one in the car, and five more at home.

AUDIE

What about your mother and father? What about them? What did they say?

JOETTA
My father…I hadn't seen my father since I was five. And, when I did he was drunk. He came in from Oklahoma one night, drunk as usual, and he and my mother got into it over supper. Sometimes, it was because there wasn't beer in the house, sometimes not. Ya never knew what it was gonna be. Anyway, he was always demanding things. This time, what my mother fixed to eat wasn't good enough, or not what he wanted, or some damn thing. She'd worked half a day on a tuna casserole dinner, and that asshole wanted Frito pies. After the screamin' and yellin' he pulled a knife outta the drawer and said in this real quiet voice, "You bitches take a good look at me, cuz I'm the last thing you're ever gonna see." He took a couple of steps toward us then he just stopped. He dropped the knife, and walked out. That's the last anyone ever saw of him. So, what I'm tellin' you is that it was just my mom and me from then on.

AUDIE
I have to ask you something. Please forgive my being indelicate. I don't know really how to say this, but….

JOETTA
I know what you're gonna ask. You're gonna ask how I knew Lacy was your father, right? Is that right?

AUDIE
How did you know? How could you know?

JOETTA
Sometimes, a mother just knows….a mother…

A COMFORT BREEZE

AUDIE
(Interrupting) Was he? Are you sure?

JOETTA
I'm sure. I didn't ask him to wear--

AUDIE
(*interrupting again*) You don't need to go any further. I know what you mean. Thank you for your honesty. (*Audie's mood changes and she becomes very distant*)

JOETTA
(*Joetta not noticing*) Maybe deep down, maybe I wanted it to happen. I somehow thought that if it did happen, if I did get pregnant, maybe he'd want me again. That it could be like it was when we were twelve or thirteen. That's the purest love, you know. That's when dreams are real, and life isn't. That's when everything is colored by feelings, and you kiss your pillow at night and pretend it's him. Have you ever loved someone so much that the smallest thought of him give you that little tingly feeling way down in your stomach? Have you? Anyway. Momma sent me up to Enid, Oklahoma. There was this "place" there where girls like me went to have…to get…well, to get things taken care of. I don't mean an abortion. Hell, it was illegal in those days, anyway. I mean to have babies sorta in a secret kinda way. It didn't cost anything, and the story was that I went away to visit a sick aunt to take care of her. Funny, everyone there was taking care of a sick aunt. After you were born…well, there was this woman who…who…I'm sorry. (*pause*) This is the part I don't wanna talk about right now. I can't talk about right now. (*another*

longer pause) Back to what I was sayin'…did you ever love someone the way I mentioned? The way I loved Lacy? I'm sure you did. You must have. All girls have that one someone who's that…that special one.

AUDIE

(*after a long pause*) No. Never. (*coldly*) That's never happened to me.

JOETTA

My god, child, you live with cold, doncha?

AUDIE

I'm going to tell you something, and I'm sure you won't like it. I live with reality, and if that's "cold", then yes. That's how I live. I'm sorry. I'm sorry for me…myself, but that's life as I know it. I pride myself in being a survivor, nothing more, nothing less. People call me cold-blooded, and you know what? I've learned to like it. That's me. That's my identity. I have this pin. This pin that has rhinestones that spell out "number one bitch" on it, and it's my favorite piece of jewelry. That's who I am. Are you disappointed?

JOETTA

But, I saw you. I saw you caring for me, concerned about me. That wasn't real? It was all an act? (*starting to cry a little*) This has all been an act? My god, I'm sorry for you. I'm really sorry for you. I gave you my life with all of the warts and bumps, and you gave me…just what did you give me? Just what WAS that?

A COMFORT BREEZE

AUDIE
(Coldly) Reality.

JOETTA
And, you don't believe in God, either. Again, how do you explain all of this? I want to understand you. If we could just--

AUDIE
And again...reality. Live with it. I do. *(Joetta, still crying silently, looks stunned. Audie stands at the edge of the stage looking out. There is no sign of any emotion on her face)*

JOETTA
Do you wanna know somethin'? You aren't a bitch, and you don't live in reality. Lookin' at you, I realize somethin'. I realize that not every ass I've seen has been hangin' over a toilet. You're just a phony. Nothing more that a fourteen Karet phony. Now, I know you. I finally know who you are. I've seen people like you all of my life. You have the looks. You have the stuff of class. You have the cars, the luggage, the jewelry, but you don't have anything real. Do you remember that I told you I always wanted to be someone? Compared to you, I am someone. I'd rather be me than you any day of the week because at least I'm real. This is what you get. I've been married four times, shacked up with I don't know how many men, and I haven't got more than two-hundred dollars between me and livin' outta my car, but you know what? I'm better than you. I remember this cat that I had once--

AUDIE
Oh, not again, please, Jesus Christ. Just not again…

JOETTA
(*angrily*) …and I loved that cat. He was mine, and before you came along he was the only thing that mattered to me. You know why? Because he didn't judge me. He didn't look at me like I was trash. Do you have any idea what that means to be someone like me? That's right…I said it, "someone like me." And, at one of the lowest points of my life, my cat got hit by a car. I saw it happen, too. I held that cat until he died, watchin' him gasp for that last breath and lookin' at me for help that wouldn't come, and that I couldn't give him. And, I wanted to die right along with him. He was my--

AUDIE
It was just a damn cat. What difference--

JOETTA
You still don't get it, do you? I couldn't help but think that the reason the cat died and I didn't was because God musta liked that cat better than he liked me. So, go ahead. Get in your goddamn 'Aleese'' or whatever you call that thing you drive and go. Get outta here. Go back to what you hold up to be important in life. (*pause*) I like me, but I don't like you. I AM better than you, Audillia. (*phone rings and Joetta picks up the receiver. Using a mock-sophisticated voice*) Hello? I do appreciate that. I dunno…I dunno if we'll need that better room or not. Well, I do so appreciate the fact that you're still workin' on it. Oh, yes, my party and I are getting along just swimmingly. Yes,

this IS Joetta Moss. Well, thank you so very much. (*hangs up*) Didja hear that? I can be a phony, too. I can sound exactly like you, just as haughty, just as "real" and just as hollow.

AUDIE
(*Coldly again*) And, am I supposed to be impressed? With your (*making finger quotation marks*) "reality"?

JOETTA
(*Coldly*) Here's (*making finger quotation marks back at her*) reality for ya. Fuck you, princess, just fuck you! (*Looks at her*) Now, you're spoze to be impressed...

> *She walks over, lights a cigarette and turns on the radio. "Just A Dream" comes on as the lights fade.*

END OF ACT I

ACT II

The music fades in. This is a continuation of ACT I. The play takes place in "real" time.

AUDIE

(*with a smirk on her face*)   You think I had that coming, don't you? You think that because I don't see your problems as something out of the ordinary, I'm unable to understand what's going on with you. Well, hold on to your green pearl luggage because I DO understand. You see, I know you, too. I know you better that anyone in the world knows you. I've seen you all of my life…in every town I've ever lived in…in every joint I've ever worked in, and in behind every counter of every dump I've ever ordered a cup of coffee in. You're everywhere. The only unique thing about you is that somehow, I was born of you. That's not good, not bad, it's just the truth.

JOETTA

Don't talk to me about truth. Don't you dare stand there and preach to me about truth. You don't have that…

AUDIE

Right? Is that what you were going to say? That I don't have that right? I have every right. You invited me here, remember? I didn't look you up. You looked me up. That gives me the right! Curiosity also gives me certain rights.

A COMFORT BREEZE

JOETTA
(angrily) Now, you lissin, cupcake. You just lissin to me for a minute or two. This started out a little awkward. Then it got okay for a little bit, there. Then, it got real damn awkward again. If I wanted to ride a roller-coaster, I'd have gone the state fair, but not here. Do you understand me? And, what's this "truth" crap, anyway? I don't think you've been honest with me since you came through that door. So, don't give me your speech about truth. You're right. I looked you up. Not the other way around. And, that gives me rights, too. It would have been a hell of a lot easier for you to tell me to fuck off, and not come here at all. So, since you're here, let's talk it out. Let's talk it out, or let's get the hell outta here, and get on with life.

AUDIE
(coldly) I'm not used to this.

JOETTA
To what?

AUDIE
Being talked to like this.

JOETTA
Well, pardon me all to hell, but I'm talkin' to you like this. And, I'm not used to tellin' my life story to a complete stranger, either. That kinda makes us kinda blood brothers, doesn't it?

AUDIE
(after a long pause) I envy you.

JOETTA
(shocked) What? Oh, please.

AUDIE
(quietly) I said that I envy you.

JOETTA
(not comprehending) Now, why in the world would someone like you envy me? How could you possibly--

AUDIE
Because you ARE real, that's why. Remember when you got so upset because I referred to you as "someone like you?" See, I always wanted to be the one people referred to as "someone like you" but in a different way. That way you just did. That way that means "she's someone special." I guess I wanted to be "something", too. We're not that much different, you and I. *(laughs a little)* I just have nicer luggage, that's all. I have a nicer watch, clothes, car, and a nicer address, but we're the same person. And, I think that's what bothers me so much. I've worked at being better than other people. That sounds terrible, doesn't it? I've worked my ass of for that. All that work, and still….

JOETTA
And, you're still just you. Is that it?

AUDIE
No, I'm still just YOU, and THAT'S it.

A COMFORT BREEZE

JOETTA
(puzzled) But, now you've...I mean.... Look, I'm sorry. That one just went right passed me.

AUDIE
Tell me about your mother.

JOETTA
What kinda switch is that? That's not even what we're talkin' about. You were sayin' that we're alike, then all of a sudden, you ask me about—

AUDIE
That's right. Tell me. Tell me about your mother. What was she like? Was she pretty? Was she nice? Was she young, old...what? What was she like?

JOETTA
(playing along) Well...well, she was young, but always seemed old. D'ya know what I mean? She was pretty at one time, I guess, but I don't remember her that way. She was always tired. Really, really tired. I remember her always wanting to lie down for a few minutes. Then, she'd lie down for hours. I didn't understand it at the time, but I guess she was always depressed or somethin'. I remember she made the best angel food cakes, though. They were so light you couldn't even feel 'em. She made 'em for my birthday every year. She always just put one candle on the cake, no matter how old I was. She said that was to show me that I was always the one person she loved. Funny, though, we were never close. We couldn't really talk, ya know? She'd just say that I should tell God about stuff, and he'd help me. *(long pause)* I

kinda think I'm due a lot of help. Anyway, I loved her, and I felt really sorry for her, bein' married to my dad, and all. But, with all of the crap he caused her, she never talked about it. Even after he took off, I was always waitin' for God to help her, too.

AUDIE
Did he?

JOETTA
No. No, he never did. Not one damn bit. She died not long after you were born. She wasn't that old, either. I think she just died from bein' tired, ya know what I mean? Maybe that was his way of helpin' her. I dunno.

AUDIE
When you got pregnant, did she help you? She must have.

JOETTA
(starts to cry a little) No. All she did was take me to Oklahoma and tell me that she'd write me, but she only wrote me one time. She told me that things were fine, and that was it. You know how she signed it? "Your mother"…that's how. Not an "I love you"… nothin'. And, I wrote her every day. After I came back home, after she died, I found my letters to her. They were all unopened. I guess that's when I realized that I was really… alone. All those months, and never a word, never a visit. It's like I'd died. Maybe to her, I was dead. I'm not sure.

A COMFORT BREEZE

AUDIE
What about Lacy? Did you ever hear from him?
JOETTA
Oh, no. Not one damn time. Oh, I did get a letter from Burt Swink. He was the Rutledge's lawyer. It said that the Rutledge family wasn't responsible in any way for you, and that no claims were to be presented by me. Burt Swink...that bastard had bruises on his forehead from ambulances hittin' their breaks too fast. Nah, after I gave you up for adoption, I was on my own. There wasn't anything in Eagle Flats. I spoze there never was. Not really. I just kinda drifted from one man to another, one marriage to another, one job to another. You know what I mean.

AUDIE
Then why did you say earlier that Lacy was a beautiful man? Did you see him? Did you ever have contact with him? How did you know? You must have--

JOETTA
I ran into a girl I'd gone to school with. She was livin' in Dallas, and I saw her at a Gibson's store. She told me that she'd heard that Lacy was back livin' in New Mexico. Well, like a fool, I gassed up my car and took off to see him. I just wanted to look at him one more time, you understand. Sure enough, there he was in Roswell. That's where all of that UFO shit's spoze to be. Anyway, I saw him, okay. He was managin' a miniature golf course. I just sat there in the car and looked at him...and looked...and looked some more.

AUDIE
So, he was the same? Was he as you remembered him?

JOETTA
Honey, that was two years ago that I saw him. A lot of time had passed both of us by. He'd probably gained about forty or fifty pounds. He was nearly bald, and he looked tired.

AUDIE
Then…he wasn't at all what you remembered?

JOETTA
(very quietly) He was exactly as I remembered. He was still the most beautiful, golden thing in the world. No…to me, he hadn't changed a bit. The years and pounds didn't matter. It was still…Lacy.

AUDIE
Why didn't you say something to him? I mean, you came all that way.

JOETTA
I dunno. He was married. Some Mexican woman, I think. At least that's what I heard. And, what d'ya say? "Hi, it's me? Let's talk about old times? It's been twenty-eight years, so what's new?" Naw. I had nothin' to say to him. I just sat in the car and watched him work on the damn elephant's trunk. You know, where the ball goes past the trunk, and ya win a free game? I watched 'til closin' time, then I just drove away. He never saw me at all. I guess that's all I needed, ya know? Just to see him one more time. But, ya know what? I still loved him just as much. Just as

much as I ever had, maybe more. Funny isn't it? That "one" love is really the only love, I guess. It's the one ya never get over, ya never can forget. But I was able to drive away. That's one of the hardest things I ever had to do, well, besides watch 'em take you away. Those were sure enough two of those "water tower" times I told you about.

AUDIE
But, at least you saw him. At least you--

JOETTA
I'll tell you somethin' kinda funny. That night, on my way outta town, I stopped to fill up the car at a gas station, and I overheard two women talkin'. One of 'em said somethin' about that guy who ran the miniature golf course, and how he was foolin' around with some big insurance man's wife. Hell, that's Lacy. I guess he hadn't changed even a little. That son of a bitch, if he had no hands and a padlock on his jeans, he still couldn't keep his fly zipped. Ya know, I kinda felt sorry for him right then. I really did. People talkin' about him behind his back, and all. He'll die from gettin' shot in some strange bed, I'll guarantee ya that. What makes some men like that? What makes 'em...

AUDIE
(*quietly*) Like every men I've ever known?

JOETTA
I'm sorry. What did you just say?

AUDIE
Nothing. I didn't say anything.

JOETTA
Yes you did. You said, "like every man I've ever known," didn't you? Didn't you say that? Cuz, I heard--

AUDIE
We're not talking about me. We're talking about...

JOETTA
Me? Not anymore, we're not. We've been talkin' about me pretty much the whole time you've been here. Do you realize that? I still don't know a damn thing about you except that you like appearin' cold, you have nice stuff, and you don't believe in God. Other than that, I'm lost as a turkey in a hail storm. Have you ever seen a turkey in a hail storm? They just stand there and get beat to death. With shelter three feet away, too. If I had to go on one of those TV game shows with a turkey or a rock a as partner, I'd choose the rock, and that's the--

AUDIE
(*totally out of the blue, and very matter of factly*) Do you know what it's like to be fucked two-thousand, one-hundred and eight-four times before your seventeenth birthday?

JOETTA
(*almost speechless and after a really long pause*) Oh, my god…what did you just—

A COMFORT BREEZE

AUDIE
(quietly) I just said--

JOETTA
(also quietly) No...I know what you said. I heard what you said. I'm just tryin' to....sweet Jesus in heaven. Please tell me that somehow you're just tryin' to shock me.

AUDIE
No, I'm not trying to--

JOETTA
This is what you meant by "fathers, uncles, brothers, cousins," is that it? You mean that they did things to you? They were the ones who—

AUDIE
There weren't any "fathers or uncles...." There were just people. People I lived with from home to home. There were just a bunch of sick, horny bastards that--

JOETTA

> *The next several lines of dialog should be very fast and overlapping. No time should be taken for pauses. The dialog isn't as important as the intent of the exchange. This should build very quickly. The chaos should end with the ring of the phone.*

(calmly) What you just said was that you've been... that... that you've been... (*screams*) Goddammit,

NO! No, please, NO! *(she falls across the bed cupping her face in her hands)* Not you, God, not her…not…*(she sobs loudly)* It's not fair, it's not…please make it go away, just make just go away. I didn't hear this... *(she is uncontrollable by now)* You bastard! You sorry bastard, why? Why her? Just kill me, please…please, please just kill me. Just make it go away, make it go away now, PLEASE…..

AUDIE

(very calmly) It started when I was three. I was--

JOETTA

(still hysterical) NO! *(putting her hands to her ears)* NO! I won't listen… I'm not listenin'… do you see me not listenin'? Tell me it isn't real, tell me it's a bad dream, a sick joke, SOMETHIN'! Please tell me that…that…

AUDIE

Damn you, you're going to listen. You're going to listen to every word I'm going to tell you. *(she grabs her hands)* Listen. Listen to me. *(Joetta still screaming)* Shut up and listen to me…NOW!

JOETTA

(gasping for breath) No, please make it go away. I'm begging you to make it go away. The clock… I'm seein' the clock right now. It's gonna be better in a minute, isn't it? Huh? Please…Isn't it? My god, I'm looking but… I can't see it. I can't see the goddamn clock… I'm lookin' but it's not there. It's gotta be there, it's gotta be…I'll kill 'em, I'll kill every

A COMFORT BREEZE 73

goddamn one of 'em. *(hysterical)* Where are they? Please. Where are they? *(she runs for the door)*

AUDIE

(going after her) Stop. Stop it now. You're not going anywhere. Just sit down. *(she sits her in the chair)* Listen to me. You're going to...*(phone rings and Audie answers)* Hello. No. No, everything's fine. No. Not at all. No, we thought we saw a rat, that's all...Well, I'm sure that there are no rats in your motel. Yes, I can see that this is a clean place. Oh yes, really one of the nicest I've ever been in *(she smiles at Joetta)*...And, you've applied to Triple A, too? I'm sure that'll be coming through any day, now. And, good luck with that. *(she hangs up)*

JOETTA

(calming down slightly) I'm okay. I'm gonna be okay. Oh, my god. *(trying to catch her breath, but still gasping)* Why did you tell me about this? Jesus...Didn't you know what I thought this weekend would be like, didn't you? Didn't you? I thought we'd have some fun, maybe shop around a little, and bullshit each other about what our lives are like. I... I had no idea it'd be like this. Not like this at all. I mean, after I found where you were, and saw where you lived, I thought that your life was... was...

AUDIE

(coldly and quietly) Glorious? Rich? Free from problems? Please, Joetta, grow up. No one has a life like that. Certainly not me. Obviously, not you. Not anyone I know. I never did ask you. Well, I never had

a chance to, really. Now, stop. Listen, but how did you find me? How were you ever able to—

JOETTA

(*calming down and lighting a cigarette*) Butch.

AUDIE

Butch? That guy you told me about before? He found me?

JOETTA

No, not at all. But, I remembered that in school he'd brag about his uncle that was a private eye in San Antonio. I don't know how I remembered that, but I did. So, I called him up, went to his office, and met with him. I'm sorry. I…let me catch my breath, please. (*pauses*) He said that for five-hundred dollars he could track you down. All I had to show him was your birth record that I kept from the place in Enid. I wasn't spoze to have it, but I took it anyway. I always had it with me. It was so damn faded from the years that you could hardly read it, but…can I have some water, please? (*Audie gets her a glass of water*) I thought he'd forgotten all about me, but about a year later, he called and told me where you were, where you lived, and all sorts of things about you. He was good at what he did, that's all I can say.

AUDIE

Are you feeling any better?

JOETTA

(*still somewhat shaken*) Yeah, yeah, I am, I'm…I'm okay. I'm fine, now. I'm better. Ya just gotta give me a minute or two, I feel like I'm tryin' to juggle water

A COMFORT BREEZE

here. I just…I just can't quite seem to manage it all. I'll be okay.

AUDIE
I almost didn't respond to your letter. I almost didn't want to see you, or to know anything about you. I'd spent the first ten years wondering who you might be, and the next twenty years trying to forget that you ever were. I damn near made it, too. Until I got your letter, I just damn near made it. Was it ego that made you look for me? Was it not knowing? What was it? I have to know. Did you really think I was going to drop my life and run to you and call you "mother"? No one could do that, not after thirty years. Do you know that I don't even know for sure how old I am? I was told that my birthday is in November, but I don't really know that. I--

JOETTA
September. September twenty second, 1963. That's your birthday. Six o'clock in the morning. By six-ten you were gone.

AUDIE
(sarcastically) Well, who says that trip wasn't worth it? I drove all this way, and waited thirty years to find out when my birthday really is. I should have--

JOETTA
Don't. Don't make fun of me. Please, not now, okay?

AUDIE
Don't you see? I'm not making fun of you. I'm making fun of me…myself. I'm the joke here. I'm

funny. I'm so damn funny that I can't stand it sometimes. Here…here's a joke for you. A woman walks into a motel room and this complete stranger says, "Hi, I'm your mother." And the woman says, "Mother? I thought mothers were supposed to be around, all of your life." And the stranger says, "Not really. Ten goddamn minutes is plenty of time." Now, that's funny. That's….Or how about this…the mother says, "Why should I stick around? I have green-pearl luggage in Wichita Falls." Don't you see? Don't you see how truly funny it all is? (*she starts a controlled cry*) I'm laughing. Why aren't you laughing, huh? Come on LAUGH! It's funny, it's--

JOETTA

It's sad. It's sad and repugnant. It's the worst thing that I could have done to you. I was told…I was assured that you were gonna to be taken care of. That you were gonna be in a good home, the kinda home that I never was gonna have. I knew that. I knew what I was, and what I was always gonna be. I didn't want that for you, not you, not…

AUDIE

Not what, Joetta? Not a mother? Not a friend? Not someone to come home to everyday? Jesus Christ, I would have come home to you, and Danny, or anyone you were involved with, rather than what I had. You selfish bitch. You decided for me? You decided how I should live? You sailed out of that place in Oklahoma because YOU thought it was best for me? Well, you go to hell. You, and your decisions, and your men, and your damn green-ass luggage. You just go straight to hell. I wasn't the one who got adopted in

A COMFORT BREEZE

Oklahoma. Does that surprise you? I wasn't the one people wanted. I wasn't the cute one. Look at me. I don't have looks. I have style, and there's a huge difference. I worked at style because that's all I had. And, you know when I realized it? On my eighteenth birthday. Oh, that's right, on what I THOUGHT was my eighteenth birthday. I remember now. That wasn't real either, was it? Thanks for telling me. No, I was the one farmed out to foster homes, well-meaning church people, kindly neighbors. Oh, and several influential people in the community. Well, do you know what those people were like? Do you? Except for one family, I was the maid, the dishwasher, the servant, and the sex object. That's right...I figured it up, and I was used as their "toy" one thousand, one hundred, and eighty four times. Those were the fathers, uncles, brothers, and cousins I told you about. I got so I could identify any kind of liquor just by the smell of it on someone's breath. And, you know, I was the one who felt guilty for what they did to me. *(pauses)* "Don't tell, Audilia, God won't like you, anymore. This is our little secret Audilia, only we need to know. Does this feel good, Audilia? Do you like it, Audilia? We'll do it again, Audilia...." *(very calm as she speaks)* I heard that kind of crap as far back as I can remember. Two, three, four times a week I heard it. And, if I was bad, I got fucked because I was bad as punishment. If I was good, I got fucked as a reward. By the time I was ten or twelve, I just got used to it. I didn't cry anymore. I didn't fight anymore. I knew it was going to happen, so I just laid there and let it happen. I had long since stopped asking God to help me. Two of the men were preachers, anyway. They were "helping" in the name of God....Or, punishing me in the name of God. Take your pick. All I knew was that helping or punishing, it was exactly the same.

JOETTA

(crying silently) But, surely there was someone who—

AUDIE

Don't talk. Shut your mouth, and don't you dare talk to me right now. (*pauses*) The only thing I had going was that I was smart. Did you know that I was valedictorian of my class? Well, I was technically valedictorian of my class. When I found out, I purposely failed a few of my tests. I did it so I wouldn't have to get up in front of people and make a speech about how "life is in front of us, and don't stare up the steps, step up the stairs" and shit like that. I denied myself money for college because I was too damn ashamed to be in front of people. Funny, I still wouldn't change that part of it, speech-wise. Anyway, I went to college, and that's when I became "me". I worked my ass off to do well, too. I took every kind of job I could get. I modeled for the art classes, I worked in a drug store. I was even a waitress once, until I dumped hot soup on a customer's lap. I was--

JOETTA

What about the one good family?

AUDIE

What?

A COMFORT BREEZE

JOETTA

The one good family you were with. I mean, didn't you tell 'em what had happened? Couldn't you go to someone and let 'em know about…about, the bad things? I'd think that--

AUDIE

Don't you know what things were like back then? It's not like now, and I'm sure there were better places, but not where I was. It was a small town, lots of small towns, and… well, it sounds a lot like Eagle Flats. No, care of orphaned kids was different then. The Donagheys really saved me, I guess. At least as much as I was willing to be saved. They had a son about my age, and he was a friend. I guess my best friend. He didn't try to… well, you know. I hadn't thought about it until now, but that was the only time I really laughed. We'd just act silly, you know? Just like twelve year olds do. We called it having laughs with two "f's". It was a nice time, it really was. He taught me to ride a bicycle. He would let me borrow his sister's bicycle and we'd go everywhere. I guess that was the only time I felt safe, when I was with him. His father had this friend I didn't like, though. It sounds stupid, but he was cruel to bugs. You know those little bugs that we used to call pill bugs? Those little armored-looking bugs that would roll up if they were threatened? They were black and, well, we called them pill bugs. I don't know what you might have called them.

JOETTA

Pill bugs.

AUDIE

Anyway, he used to sit out on his patio in the mornings, and eat bags of chocolate chips like you make cookies with. It was cool, and those little bugs would be everywhere. When one would crawl by, he would slowly mash it to death with his foot. He'd just keep eating and talking, and mash those poor bugs. I hated to see him do that. It was just so, I don't know, such a methodical way to kill something. I hadn't thought about that in years, not until now, really. *(pauses)* So, these bugs were just walking to their deaths. I wanted to yell at him to stop, but I couldn't say anything. I just watched, and begged them in my mind to go around, or go somewhere else, but they kept coming, just walking toward him to be mashed into the concrete.

JOETTA

But…why those bugs? Why was that such a big thing with you? It was bad, but--

AUDIE

In one of the places I lived, there was this field out in back of the house. There must have been thousands of those pill bugs. I remember that the first time I was on the honor roll in school there was no one to really tell about it. I just sat in the field and told the bugs that I was smart, that I was on the honor roll. There were no friends, no family, just no one, so I told the bugs. I'd build little houses for them out of sticks, and gum wrappers. They were kind of like, I don't know, kind of like a big family to me. I guess I was maybe ten or eleven. This all makes me sound crazy, but--

JOETTA

No, no it doesn't, not at all. I guess those bugs were to you what my old cat was to me. Sometimes ya just need somethin' to get you through. What happened to the boy? The one you were friends with?

AUDIE

He and his family moved to Montana. His father worked for the government. He was in the Indian Affairs office, and they moved around a lot. I never heard from him after that. They were always moving, I guess. I was shuffled from one town to another... new family... new situation... you know.

JOETTA

Surely, not every family was the same. They couldn't have been...could they? I mean...

AUDIE

Sometimes it was the families, sometimes the people around the families. I was just a way for state money to come in. Nothing more. That's all I was, just an income. Look, I'm not going to go into detail about every person that...well...every person who did things to me. I got past that. It took years, but one day, I finally got past it. Okay, it also took thousands of dollars in counseling fees, but I made it. And, you know something? It all seems like it was someone else, not me that went through it. Experience, my dear woman, is a valuable lesson. Maybe it was for a purpose. Maybe it was...

JOETTA

No it wasn't.

AUDIE
What do you mean?

JOETTA
No one should hafta swim through a mile of shit for a lesson. No lesson's worth that.

AUDIE
No, you're wrong. It made me tough. It made me able to give the world the finger each and every morning when I wake up. That's worth something to me.

JOETTA
Funny, isn't it? I wake up, and think that this may be the day. This may be the brass ring day, and you wake up thinking that once again, no one's gonna screw with me, or there'll be hell to pay from everyone.

AUDIE
Don't give me that. You're the one who looks for water towers.

JOETTA
Yeah, but between the water tower times, I look for something maybe kinda good that I can comb outta life. Can't you do that? Are you capable of that?

AUDIE
(*losing her patience*) This is the life I want! I have everything I want, everything that I--

JOETTA
You have a hole in your heart where honor ought to be. That's what you've got. A great big hole that can't

A COMFORT BREEZE

be filled with Rolls Royces or anything else. I'm sad for you. I'm sadder for you than I ever was for myself.

AUDIE
Why? Why be sad for me? I'm over the bad things.

JOETTA
You thrive on the bad things. I can tell that from talkin' to you. You live with bad things and you're gonna make the world suffer right along with you. Roll in the dirt with the rich girl, that's what we're all spoze ta do. Your husband must be--

AUDIE
Leave him out if this.

JOETTA
No. I'm not gonna do it. He must be miserable to hafta--

AUDIE
It's not like that. That's not what we have going.
JOETTA
How does he live with you? Do you give him this ice princes act every day? Does he hafta put up with this?

AUDIE
(quietly) He doesn't care.

JOETTA
(pauses) He what?

AUDIE
He doesn't care, okay? He has his life. I have mine.

JOETTA
But--

AUDIE
Look, we live together, that's all. We show up together when we have to. We make each look good. Let me explain this to you. I told you that I created myself. I created myself into this. I read every book I could find about style and what was fashionable. I was going to be whatever I needed to be in order to get what I wanted. I knew that I couldn't get to where I wanted to be, by being some used up foster kid…so I worked my ass off to be what you're looking at right now. My husband makes more money in six months than most people see in a lifetime, and I make almost that much, as well. We do just fine, and that's the way we like it. All I ask for is a "position" in the community, and in return, he doesn't ask for sex, or kids, or home baked cookies. That's what I got from learning "style" and I worked damn hard to get it. We live in a seven-thousand square foot house in the quarter and it's loaded with Millard furniture. And, I sure as hell couldn't have gotten that if I'd stayed what I was. I worked at it and I'm damn proud of it.

JOETTA
So, it's all an act. You're nothin' more than an actress playin' a part--

A COMFORT BREEZE

AUDIE

You're goddamn right it's an act! I'm the best damn actress you've ever seen. I should win an Oscar every year for how good an actor I am. There's no one better, Joetta, no one better at this than I am.

JOETTA

God, I'm sorry for you.

AUDIE

Don't be sorry for me. Be sorry for you, that you didn't think of this before it was all too late.

JOETTA

So, your husband…he knows about--

AUDIE

My past? Not at all. He thinks I was an orphan. We met after college when we were both becoming successful. He doesn't ask. I don't volunteer. It works out kind of nice that way. And, I didn't tell him I was coming here to meet my long lost mother. He thinks I'm on a buying trip, that's all. All he requires of me is brain power, and class. All I require of him is a life that I used to only dream of. So, don't feel sorry for me. Be proud that I'm someone who's learned to glide between the hail stones of life. Nothing gets to me. Nothing at all. I'm re-invented, don't you see? That three year old sex object is like she never existed. Instead….

JOETTA

Instead, what? Huh? What? I'm lookin' at exactly what I was afraid that I saw before…a….Oh, never mind, Audie. It's all been said. I'm tired. This makes me tired. You make me tired. (*calmly*) Ya know somethin'....I'd kill myself before I'd let things happen to you like they did. I really would. If I thought there was a chance in hell that you would grow up like you...like you did, I'd lay down in front of a train to keep it from happenin'. It rips my heart out to hear all of the things you've told me. I guess, in a way, I AM proud of you, all that you did to improve yourself, to make things good, to make things....right for yourself. But, Christ on a crutch, is what you are really right for you? Is it? Is it really right for anyone? I wonder. I wonder 'till I'm just all wondered out...just all--

AUDIE

I'm tired, too. Now, there are two of us who know all about me, and that's one more than I ever wanted to know. My life's not so unique. It's not at all. I went to an encounter group once as part of my counseling. There were fifteen other people there who had all been through pretty much the same thing I'd been through. Different faces, different sexes, but just the same. They were all these quivering bags of Jell-O, and none of them were going to do a damn thing about where they were in life. That's when I decided that I could sit there and juggle sacks of air with them, or get off my ass and do something about it. I never went back, but I sure as hell did something about it. They were weak...all so damn weak...(*pauses*) For a long time, I'd sleep on my left side because I saw this old movie once where someone said that sleeping on your left side wore the heart out faster. Then, I realized that I had too much to live for. I was going to shove Audilia Brousard down the throats of everyone I could find, and make them like it, too.

JOETTA

Once, a long, long time ago, I was in California. I'd gone out there with some man... and... well, that's not important. We took one of those movie studio tours, and I realize that I'm taking another one right now. Everything was made of cardboard, and one layer deep, just like you. Nothing was permanent. Nothing had any substance. It was all real flashy and sparkly, but held together with bailin' wire and glue. It looked great on the surface, though. *(she slowly circles and looks at Audie)*

AUDIE

What are you talking about?

JOETTA

(still circling) You know exactly what I'm talkin' about, doncha?

AUDIE

What are you doing?

JOETTA

Lookin' for the wire and glue, sweetcakes. It's gotta be there, somewhere. I guess you just hide the seams better than some, but they're around. I know they're around. You're good. You're really good. I can't see any seams at all, but we both know, don't we? Yep, if a good hard rain came along, you'd just melt away. Just--

AUDIE
You bore me.

JOETTA
And, you don't bore me?

AUDIE
This extant attitude of condescension is wearing thin, Joetta.

JOETTA
Oooohhh, big words. Really sorta big-like words. Now, I'm intimidated. You're saying that my still existing attitude of talking down to you is wearing thin? Gosh, I'm so glad I was able to deliver an exegesis of what you were saying to me. Otherwise, I'd have been so fuckin' lost. Thank you, my dear. My dictionary's out in the car. Should I bring it in so that I might follow your sorta big-like word conversation? Your verbal gymnastics are just so damn impressive. (*pause*) Don't head down that path. You won't win, and I don't wanna hear it. Talk to me, but not down to me. Okay? Do you understand? I've had most of forty-seven years of talkin' down, and it's a little old at this point. Now, are we past boring each other? (*getting in one more dig*) Or, shall we continue the prolixity of this conversation?

AUDIE
(*still taunting Joetta*) Je ne comprends pas.

JOETTA
Oh, don't give me that bullshit. You understand everything I'm saying. I'm not an ignorant woman,

A COMFORT BREEZE

Audilia, just a little bit un-schooled, that's all. Now, are you ready to stop the word sparring because, quite frankly, you know what? It bores me. Can I ask you something? (*Audie sits silently*) And, you don't hafta answer, but I've gotta know. Have you ever enjoyed life? Has there ever been anything that made you happy? Because you—

AUDIE
"Happy" is a relative word.

JOETTA
No it's not. "Happy" is just a word, that's all. You make it relative by attachin' baggage to it. No, I just wanna know. What is it that's ever made you happy? There's gotta be sometin'. For me it was always bein' able to laugh. My god, I was always the biggest pushover for anyone who made me laugh. Men, women, kids, anyone who could make me just kick back and let loose with a big 'ol belly laugh, ya know? I'd fall for that like an egg from a tall chicken. I really would. I'd just...

AUDIE
(quietly) Historical places.

JOETTA
I'm sorry. Did you say--

AUDIE
I said, historical places. I guess I love historical places. The older, the better. The more history, the better. I love that dank smell of really old places...houses, buildings, anything like that. That

sounds funny, I know, but that's my weakness. I don't know why, but…

JOETTA
Yes you do. You know why. Tell me.
AUDIE
No, I don't…really, I don't. Maybe I think that whatever went on in those places was…nice. Maybe everyone was happy, and maybe (*catches herself*) Look…I don't have to do this. Who gives a damn about this kind of stuff? What are you, an analyst? Do you have a shingle hanging out somewhere? I didn't even mean it. I don't care about old things. I don't care about anything. What I am is what I am…nothing more, all right? I didn't mean to say that I had a weakness, either. I'm not weak. I've never been weak. I've got a headache, a really bad headache.

JOETTA
Here, I have somethin' in my suitcase that'll take care of that right away. Let me just….(*goes to her suitcase*)
AUDIE
No, I have something. I have something the doctor prescribed for me. (*she moves to her suitcase and takes out a small bottle*)

JOETTA
What is that?

AUDIE
Nothing. It's just something that makes me feel better. I've been taking it for years. It helps.

A COMFORT BREEZE

JOETTA
Do you get headaches often? I mean does this happen a lot? I just take regular 'ol aspirin. That and maybe a cold beer. Seems to work for me.

AUDIE
This is fine. (*takes her pills*) See? I'll be fine in a minute or two. Can we just talk about something calming for a change?

JOETTA
Sure we can. You start. You talk about whatever you wanna talk about and I'll just lissin. How's that? Anything, anything at all is fine with me.

AUDIE
How about you talk, and I'll listen?

JOETTA
Nope, new rules. You talk. I lissin. (*long pause*) Well, go ahead, .talk away. I'm right here. (*Audie doesn't respond*) Yep, I'm just sittin' here, just waitin'.... just, you know, waitin' around....and lissnin'....and ...waitin'. Here I am. Your turn....

AUDIE
This isn't going away if you're talking all the time.

JOETTA
That's what I'm sayin'....you talk. I'm just here because I'm no place else.

AUDIE
(*after a long painful pause*) A rhino's horn is made of hair. Okay? That's something we can talk about.

JOETTA
Well, actually, it's hair that's formed with this glue-like substance that the rhino secretes. It gets all hard, and forms what we call a horn, but it's really hair. You're right. *(laughs)* See? We have all kinds of things we can talk about, don't we?

AUDIE
And a possum has--

JOETTA
It's technically "o'possum" but go ahead.

AUDIE
I don't want to do this. All I was doing was talking about a couple of damn animals, and you have to…

JOETTA
What? I hafta what?

AUDIE
Interject with things you know. I was just—

JOETTA
How's your headache?

AUDIE
What?

JOETTA

I said, "How's your headache?"

AUDIE

(surprised) It's gone. It's…well, I'll be damned, it's gone.

JOETTA

That's a trick I learned from Dudley Boddlin. Ya get someone sidetracked from their headache, and it just goes away. Yeah, Dudley ran a bicycle shop in San Angelo. He called his place, "Blazing Straddles" kind of a take-off on the movie, I guess. He could get people goin' faster that anyone I ever knew, but he sure could cure a headache. All someone had to do was talk about anything in the world, and Dudley would start throwin' in superfluous crap, and he'd get 'em so mad and upset that they'd forget all about what they'd talked about in the first place. He was a real nice 'ol boy, though. Never made a dime in the bicycle business, but everyone just loved him. I think people would go into his shop just to see what he was gonna get started. Half the town used to hang around there. He drank Old Crow. Called it his cough medicine… by noon he was lit up like an Aggie bonfire, but he was sure a nice guy. One day, he just quit drinkin'. Said that he wasn't thirsty anymore, and just put it down. He died at his shop on Christmas Eve. He was fixin' up some old bikes to take to needy kids. No one knew it, but used to give away bikes to kids in town that didn't have any money. I think that's why he never made a buck in the bike business. He'd give ya anything he had, a good 'ol boy, for sure. He gave me a bicycle built for two, once. Just gave it to me. I was kinda down on my luck, and he told me that if I ever found anyone that I liked well enough to take the other seat, I'd be ready. I still miss him.

AUDIE
(smiling) I knew someone like that once. I really did.

JOETTA
Well, tell me about him.

AUDIE
It was a woman. She used to work at the gallery in the summers to make extra money. She was really pretty, and so nice to everyone. She taught school, but as long as I knew her, she thought she was a failure. She was divorced and had a difficult time dealing with it, but it never showed. She'd put on this great face to everyone, and… just, no one knew. No one ever knew that she was suffering. She would laugh, and make jokes, but she always thought of herself as "just a teacher." Can you imagine? I thought that being a teacher was something nice, something of accomplishment, but she never did. She wanted to be thought of as a bigger deal, I guess. She was like Dudley, I suppose. She just had something in her that made her want to give back. I think the reason she worked another job was so that she could get things for kids who needed more than what they had at home. See, when you went there, you saw the fun side of New Orleans. Not many people see the areas where poverty is a way of life, and where need is so constant. I saw it once. It kind of makes your heart break for those people, but….I don't know. You think, "Why not do something about it? Get off of

A COMFORT BREEZE

your asses and just do something more?" Do you know what I mean? They just sit there, and do nothing about their situation. Anyway, this girl worked for us for a few summers, and then...

JOETTA
Then, what?

AUDIE
I don't know. She just disappeared. But, I remember how kind she was, how nice to everyone she was. And, it wasn't that, and I hate to use the word because of what we went through a while ago, but not that phony salutation you've come to expect in shops like ours. When she greeted someone, she really meant that she was glad to see them, or...have a nice day, meant that she really wanted the people to have a nice day.

JOETTA
Didn't you try to find out what happened to her? Surely, you tried--

AUDIE
Why? She was gone. She didn't even bother to pick up her last paycheck. She worked on commission, and she had quite a lot coming, too.

JOETTA
Then, something happened to her.

AUDIE
Now, how do you know that?

JOETTA
I know. I know things like that.

AUDIE
That's just ridiculous. You don't know. You didn't even know her until I told you about her. You can't saw that something happened to her.

JOETTA
Well, it did. Trust me. Didn't you bother to look for her? Did you call anyone?

AUDIE
She left. That's it. End of story. What's the big deal, anyway?

JOETTA
Doncha see? That's what I'm talkin' about. Someone you liked, and maybe even admired in a strange way goes missin', and you just chalk it up to, "Well, she left. That's it. End of story." Dammit, Audie, doncha see a pattern, here? Doncha? Can you see that—

AUDIE
(*getting angry*) Can I see what? That someone who worked for me years ago, took off one day? That she didn't want to sell art works anymore? Please… does everything have to be an issue with you? Haven't we been down this road before? Well, I think we have, and I'm not going to bring back a monumental headache just to sift through shit again with you. My god, just let it go, can you? Well, can you? I wish I'd never have come here. I really do.

JOETTA

(*very quietly*) I'll betcha aren't gonna see this one comin', but…I love you, Audilia. God, help me, but for some reason, I do love you. It can't be your personality, and it sure as hell isn't your charm, and it's not that I'm your mother. But I for some reason that I'll never be able to explain, if I live to be a hundred, I love you.

> *Audie sits stunned in the chair. Joetta looks at her as the lights fade to black.*

END OF ACT II

ACT III

The lights come up as Audie and Joetta are in the same positions they were in before.

AUDIE

Are you saying that you respect me, too? Because you can respect someone that you don't love, but you can't love someone that you don't respect. I firmly believe that.

JOETTA

I guess I do, in an odd way. I guess I do respect you. Oh, not for who you are, and I'm sorry for that, but for pullin' yourself outta shit. Yeah. I do respect you. Not many people coulda done that the way you did. So, yes, I respect you.

AUDIE

(sarcastically) Do you love me as much as you still love Lacy? *(silence from Joetta)* Because that's more love than anyone deserves. So, where am I? Am I equal? A little bit below equal? A little bit above? Just where am I? Oh, you can tell me. After all, you love me. I am right, aren't I? You love me?

JOETTA

(pulling a very old, faded piece of paper out of her purse) I've carried this around with me for thirty-two years, and I've never shown it to anyone. You're the last person I'd wanna see it, but I'm gonna show it to you, anyway. Why? Because I think you need to see it. I'll explain it all later.

A COMFORT BREEZE

AUDIE
(taking the paper) What is this?

JOETTA
Just read it. Don't say anything. Just read the damn thing.

AUDIE
It's all faded, and--

JOETTA
READ IT! Read it, and keep your mouth shut after you do.

AUDIE
(after reading the paper) My god….

JOETTA
I said to keep your mouth shut. *(taking the paper from her)*

AUDIE
It's very pretty in its way, and more than that….very sad.

JOETTA
It's sappy as hell is what it is, but I never meant anything any more than I meant that. I still do. God, I can't stand it, but I do.

AUDIE
(Quoting) "Take all of the love in the universe, multiply it by infinity, and that's but a fraction of

what I feel for you." I'm impressed. I'm very impressed. You have a poet's heart.

JOETTA
No. I have a schoolgirl's memory. I wanted you to read it because I hope you can find that kinda love someday… somewhere. I hope you can.

AUDIE
It won't happen, but I appreciate you sharing it with me. And, I appreciate you showing me where I fall on the love scale.

JOETTA
Don't call it that.

AUDIE
What, the love scale? But, that's what it is, isn't it? Just a way for you to measure where we all fit. How your love is doled out? I just read Lacy's love letter. I saw that, but where was Danny? Where was Butch? Hell, I'm sure that Ernesto was there, too… wasn't he? Where did he fit? Tell me… How about every high school boy in Eagle Flats, huh? Just, where do we all fit?

JOETTA
Do you hafta make everything so common? Do you? Do you hafta poison life for everyone around you? My god, are you that jaded that everything and everyone is categorized? Do you compartmentalize life that much? You have the brass ring, but you don't see it, do you? You pathetic misfit--

AUDIE

Pathetic misfit! Why in the hell am I a pathetic misfit? I OWN the brass ring, dear. You...You're still grabbing for it. I created the goddamn brass ring, and it's mine, exclusively. And, I don't share it with anyone.

JOETTA

And, what is it? Just what is the brass ring to you? Is it the car and the crap that goes with it? It's gotta be the big 'ol house, too. What about the Millard furniture? That's gotta play into the mix. I'll tell you something...When you're tired, a bed with an egg carved into the headboard doesn't sleep any better than a bed from Sears. And, I've been dog-ass tired a bunch of times when an army cot slept just fine, too. So, see? Your brass ring shit is just like mine. Or maybe it's not. The only thing different is the price tag.

AUDIE

Then, what's your brass ring? What makes that ephemeral brass ring of yours so lofty, huh? I think that "working man's ethic" that you accused me of having is coming in to play again, don't you?

JOETTA

It's not "ephemeral" at all. And, it's not lofty, Audilia. My brass ring is long-lastin', corny, simple, and what I value out of life. You wouldn't understand. You're transparent. You could be wearin' a suit of armor, and concrete underwear, and I could still see through you. (*pauses*) I guess my brass ring is an old couple whose fingers are so swollen that you just know they haven't had their wedding rings off for years. It's a kid with a broken arm with a cast full of signatures from all of his friends. It's someone who still believes that Santa Claus is coming to visit, and the Easter bunny really does leave candy at night. It's givin' a stray animal a bite of food to help it along. It's seein' shapes in the clouds, and a New Mexico sunset. It's a real west Texas comfort breeze. It's knowin' that laughs… maybe even those with two "F's" like you talked about are gonna be out there, somewhere. It's an old cook named Ernesto throwin' you a towel to cry into when you need it the most. That's the brass ring. That's my brass ring, anyway. You don't get it, do you? I might just as well be explainin' sex to a chicken as to get this across to you. Am I right?

AUDIE
(smirks) That's it? That's the brass ring to you? Those sound nice, but they're just things that are already around. There's nothing remarkable about any of that. Nothing grand, or magic, or unique about anything you mentioned.

JOETTA
(quietly) I know. I know that, and that's the charm of it, doncha see? It's just the everyday stuff that I always wanted, but never found enough of. I grabbed for it all of my life, and I only got it in short bursts. I think the difference between us is that you could have so easily had those things. Because of my choices, I never could…not for long, anyway. So, I guess you're right. It is my ephemeral brass ring. Maybe, it always has been nothing more than that. And, maybe…maybe, you do know me better than I

thought. I'm transparent, too. I know that. But, I told you… this is whatcha get. This is the "Joetta experience"…. right here.

AUDIE
(quietly) And, the "Audie experience" is what? Sitting in a gallery selling paintings that look like they were done by six year olds in art class? Is that what you're suggesting?

JOETTA
Who said anything about art? We weren't talkin' about "art" at all. Where'd you get that?

AUDIE
You know where I work, what I do. Well, I'll tell you something, the art works I sell are in some of the finest homes in the country. *(becoming very defensive)* Some very important people buy from me, and it took years to get my reputation….

JOETTA
I'm not belittling what you do. All I was sayin' is that your brass ring and mine are obviously different. Grow up. Just please grow--

AUDIE
The paintings, and art work that I broker are from some of the greatest--

JOETTA
Do they look like anything real? Well, do they?

AUDIE
(angry) Does WHAT look like anything real?

JOETTA
Those damn art works. Are they squiggles on a sheet of canvas, or do they actually look like something?

AUDIE
Art is subjective, Joetta. Art is--

JOETTA
Bullshit! Art is what someone's willin' to buy, and call it a masterpiece, that's all. There was some asshole in New York who'd found the next Rembrandt, and he was sellin' his crap for a fortune. Ya know who the artist turned out to be? A monkey…a goddamn monkey. Now, what's it worth to have Mr. Muggs whip up a painting for ya, huh? Lotsa "art" folks had egg on their faces over that one. Or, should I say bananas on their faces?

AUDIE
It's called modern art, Joetta and it looks--

JOETTA
(interrupting) Like hammered shit. Admit it. Paint thrown in canvas, and stretched out Pepsi bottles aren't art. Women with six breasts? People with lopsided eyes? Rooms that look like the fun house at the state fair's floor plan? C'mon, it's crap. *(smiles at Audie)* Isn't it? Huh? Huh? Come on, just tell 'ol Joetta. Just repeat after me, "Yeah, it looks like…"

AUDIE
(laugh a little) Shit. Okay, a lot of it looks like shit, but—

A COMFORT BREEZE

JOETTA
(laughs out loud) Good for you. Just good for you. Now, that's honest, and ya know what? That's real. There's hope for you, yet. By the time you leave here, you'll be lookin' at those pictures of Elvis on black velvet and sayin', "Ya know, that's some pretty damn good stuff."

AUDIE
Oh, I've developed an appreciation for some of it. It keeps me in beignets, I guess. Some of it's really pretty in its own way.

JOETTA
So, what will you do when you leave? Are you gonna travel around before you go home, or just head straight back? What didja have in mind? I have this place booked for three nights, and--

AUDIE
I don't know. I'll look around. If I buy something, I can write the trip off. I'd like to see New Mexico. Maybe I'll go to Santa Fe. Maybe I'll go--

JOETTA
Santa Fe? That's where ya need to be. They have crap there that's way too over-priced, so you just might fit in real nice there. *(she laughs)*

AUDIE
(ignoring her) I've never seen it, and the pictures look wonderful. I just might spend some time there. Maybe look to open another gallery…

JOETTA
(quietly) You're not gonna stay here for all three days, are you?

AUDIE
(pauses) No, Joetta, I'm not. I can't.

JOETTA
You can't, or you won't. There's a big difference.

AUDIE
I won't. I'm sorry.

JOETTA
(saving face) Well, hell….I kinda knew you wouldn't. I've got things to do, too. I have places to go, and lotsa people to see about. What is it that Robert Frost said? "Miles to go before I sleep?" That's me. Miles to go before I sleep. I may drive down to Midland, anyway. There's this ol' boy I knew one time, and I just might look him up. He had a motorcycle, and I've always been a sucker for any guy on a motorcycle. He had this pet raccoon that'd ride on his bike with him. Had little goggles that he'd made for him, and the two of 'em would just take off for anywhere the road would lead 'em. I remember one time Lonnie Jr., that was his name, and that raccoon were ridin' down Main Street and Lonnie Sr. ran out of his store and started yellin' and screamin' at him to ….*(pause)*

AUDIE
What's the matter? Why did you stop?

A COMFORT BREEZE

JOETTA
(a long pause) The stories are over, Audie. There aren't any more stories. I'm storied out for right now. I'm storied out for a long time to come. Maybe I've told 'em all. Maybe….

AUDIE
I…I don't understand.

JOETTA
I think you do. Look, I've had forty-seven years of tellin' stories about people I know, things I did, things I wanted to do. My life's become a quilt of faceless people, and at some point they all become the same…the same person. And, if I live to be a hundred, all I'm gonna do is add more pieces to the quilt. More stories, more adventures, more memories that no one but me cares about. I've seen 'em all before and I've experienced 'em all before. I guess I'm just like Momma was. I'm just tired. But, I've been tired for the last thirty years, so what's new? Every time I round a corner, I think that this is gonna be home for me. This is gonna be the place that I can just take off my shoes and put my feet up for a while, but it never is. I used to say that Daddy musta been a Gypsy and Momma musta been a nomad cuz I always had the bug just to move on.

AUDIE
It's funny. All I wanted to do was stay in one place. I guess that's from being shuffled off so much when I was young.

JOETTA
That's not funny at all. I know exactly what you're talkin' about. I understand what you mean. See, I "get it" more than people think I do.

AUDIE
I know. I know you do.

JOETTA
Lissin. I want you to have somethin'. *(she takes a piece of paper and hands it to Audie)*

AUDIE
It's your note about Lacy. The one about how much you love him. I can't take this.

JOETTA
No, you take it. You just go on and take it with you. You might need it someday. I hope that one day you'll feel that way about someone. Take it. Please.

AUDIE
But--

JOETTA
It's okay. I'm ready to let go of it. I think I can, now.

AUDIE
Are you all right?

JOETTA
(*covering her feelings*) You bet I am, sugar. (*laughs really loud*) I'm just solid as a government dime. Take it. I mean it. Okay? I'm fine, really. Hell, if I can't

A COMFORT BREEZE

give my own daughter somethin', then who can I give it to? I don't need it, not anymore. Besides, it's weighin' me down. Maybe it has been for a lot of years, ya know? (*pause*) I've got things to do. Yessir, lotsa things to do. (*crying silently*) Now, you take it, or I'm gonna just throw it right in the trash. How 'bout that?

AUDIE
(*quietly*) Well,.all right. Thank you. This is very nice.

JOETTA
Nice, hell. (*still covering*) I'm not nice at all. I'm "real"…remember? Someone very special to me told me that one time.

AUDIE
(*laughs a little*) And, someone told me that I was a phony. Remember?

JOETTA
Someone "special" to you, or just someone?

AUDIE
(*pauses and smiles*) I think someone special. (*Audie starts gathering her belongings*)

JOETTA
You goin' somewhere?

AUDIE
(*quietly*) Yes, Joetta…I am. It's time for me to leave.

JOETTA
Aww, hell. I knew you wouldn't stay for long. I have this place booked for a coupla more days, now. And, you're sure welcome to--

AUDIE
(interrupting) No, it's time. When I first got here, I was wondering how I was going to leave. Now, I know. I'm going to leave between the stories, the fights, the phone calls from the desk, and the ill feelings. I think that's best.

JOETTA
By damn, ya may be right. Just leave while it's all good. That's best. That works for me, too. (*turning her face away and after a very long pause)* Will I ever see you again?

AUDIE
I'm not saying that we'll never see each other again, but….

JOETTA
(*quietly)* Never's a long time.

AUDIE
Probably not. This isn't something I say to hurt you. I don't want that, really, but I just think that--

JOETTA
You're right. Anyway, you know me. Here one day, somewhere else the next. Naw, when you're like me, ya just gotta keep movin'. It's what I do, I guess. I kinda like it that way, though.

A COMFORT BREEZE

AUDIE
You know something? You're like no one I've ever known before. I like you, Joetta. I really like you. And, I admire you. You're plucky, and I like that in people.

JOETTA
Well, I am that. Hey, tell me somethin'. What are ya gonna tell folks about this get-together? I mean, are ya gonna tell 'em that you met me, or...what?

AUDIE
No. This is ours. No one needs to know besides just us. This is ours alone. What about you? What will you say?

JOETTA
(laughs) I'm gonna say that I know someone who drives a Rolls Royce, and let it go at that. Let 'em just wonder about it.

AUDIE
(moves toward the door) Well...This is...I guess...goodbye. *(offering her hand)*

JOETTA
Oh, c'mon...you can do better that that. *(hugs her a long hug)* Now, that's better isn't it? You go on, now. You just get on the road. *(starts to cry a little)* You get outta here before that plaster falls down on you, or somethin'. Remember, now, if you ever wanna hear some of those good ol' west Texas stories, ya know where to come.

AUDIE

(*opening the door, and as she exits*) I'll know exactly where to come. *(starts to cry a little as she exits)* I'll never forget you. If I live to be a hundred, I'll…. (*exits*)

JOETTA

Looking around the room slowly. She cries quietly as she mixes a drink. She goes to her razor, and looks at it for a few seconds then puts it in her suitcase. She looks out the window as she hears Audie's car drive away. She sits on the bed and the phone rings.

Hello. No, everything's fine. Really? When? How long? Well, that's sweet of you, but I won't need it now. No, this one's just fine. That's right….I'll just keep the room I'm in. I know what I said, but this one's okay after all. Well, I know, but I was different then. Now, I'm just plucky… Well, look it up. Maybe you'll find an exegesis of it. Look that one up, too. Oh, and lissin…Where's a good place to eat around here? Okay. Thanks.

Hangs up. Joetta carefully looks through her things. She finishes her drink. She places her suitcase on the bed, and washes the glasses. She even straightens the bedspread. She picks up the phone.

Say, I wanted to ask you somethin'... (*after a short pause*) Where's the closest water tower? (*lights start to fade*) Yeah (*sighs*) that's what I said. Uh huh, water tower.... *(reaches over and turns on the radio and all that's on is static)*

CURTAIN

www.ingramcontent.com/pod-product-compliance
Lightning Source LLC
Chambersburg PA
CBHW071742080526
44588CB00013B/2126